A Dog and A Clock

A Dog and A Clock

... And 30 Other Bible-Based Meditations

Roger Ellsworth

Unless otherwise noted, Scripture quotations are taken from the New King James Version®. Copyright © 1982 by Thomas Nelson. Used by permission. All rights reserved.

Copyright © 2017, Roger Ellsworth

All rights reserved. No part of this book may be reproduced, scanned, or distributed in any printed or electronic form without permission.

First Edition: 2017

978-0-9988812-9-4

LS20170425

Great Writing Publications
www.greatwriting.org
Taylors, SC

www.greatwriting.org

Purpose

My Coffee Cup Meditations are short, easy-to-read, engagingly presented devotions based on the Bible, the Word of God. Each reading takes a single idea or theme and develops it in a thought-provoking way so that you are inspired to consider the greatness of God, the relevance of the good news of the life, death, resurrection, and coming-again of Jesus, and are better equipped for life in this world and well prepared for the world to come.

www.mycoffeecupmeditations.com

https://www.facebook.com/MyCoffeeCupMeditations/

Dedication

Dedicated to Jackie and Amy Vaughan

(Philippians 1:3-5)

Table of Contents

1 A dog and a clock 16
2 Whenever I am afraid 20
3 He to rescue me from danger 24
4 Tell me what you think you owe 28
5 The passing of a celebrity 32
6 Two questions most church attendees dare not ask 36
7 Christianity or "Ianity"? 40
8 The danger of snapshot theology 44
9 Cookie, the Christmas dog 48
10 And the award for best-dressed goes to 52
11 Vacationing in a cemetery 56
12 Who is really relevant? 60
13 Something we should all desire 64
14 Bethlehem's Well 68
15 "Why this waste?" 72
16 The dying thief rejoiced to see that fountain 76
17 Why does Christianity seem to mean so little? 80
18 What to preach on Easter 84
19 What about hypocrites in the church? 88
20 Finding God's will 92
21 How can we be sure God exists? 96

22 Just call me Barabbas 100
23 A crisis of faith 104
24 Weird things.. 108
25 When it happens... 112
26 Savoring 116
27 "Trusting in my Father's wise bestowment".................. 120
28 Turtles all the way down 124
29 True riches 128
30 Things I miss 132
31 Astonishing Love 136

About the Author 141

The App

www.mycoffeecupmeditations.com/app

(Coming soon)

Be sure you get the app!

-1-

From God's Word, the Bible...

Do not fear any of those things which you are about to suffer. Indeed, the devil is about to throw some of you into prison, that you may be tested, and you will have tribulation ten days. Be faithful until death, and I will give you the crown of life.

Revelation 2:10

A Dog and A Clock

Being a lover of dogs, I was moved by these lines I came across from an old issue of a Christian news magazine that I was reading:

> *The dog of Angelo del Plato watched intently as his master was lowered into the grave. Eight years later, friends of the family acknowledged that they could not remember a day when that loving dog did not visit his master's gravesite, usually sitting a while on the turf over his master's body.*

Even those who are not dog lovers must admire and commend the faithfulness of that dog to his master. It is a sharp rebuke to many Christians for their lack of faithfulness to their Master!

Yes, all Christians have a Master—the Lord Jesus Christ! Tell me that you do not regard Jesus as your Master, and I will not hesitate to tell you that you are not a Christian! I do so on no less authority than that of the Apostle Paul: "If anyone does not love the Lord Jesus Christ, let him be accursed …" (1 Cor. 16:22).

I'm sure that Angelo del Plato did much to win the affection of his dog. He undoubtedly fed him, talked to him, played with him, walked with him, and cared for him when he was sick.

The question I have for my fellow-believers is simply this: Has your Master, the Lord Jesus Christ, done less for you than del Plato did for his dog? Every Christian must immediately utter a resounding "No!" to that question. The Lord Jesus has done infinitely more for us than del Plato did for his dog! The Lord Jesus has rescued us from the wrath of God by receiving that wrath in our stead. He has forgiven us of our sins. He has made us part of the family of God. He has given us countless blessings and benefits to make life more comfortable and pleasant. And He has promised to eventually take us home to Himself to share in His eternal glory. What more could the Lord Jesus do for us?

We should frequently remind ourselves of these words from Jesus: "But why do you call me 'Lord, Lord,' and do not do the things which I say?" (Luke 6:46).

The issue facing each of us is whether we will be as faithful to our Master as del Plato's dog was to him. Or will we commend in a dog that which we refuse to practice ourselves?

My wife and I have moved a lot in our years together. One item always receives special attention when we move. It is our Seth Thomas clock. I awoke a few minutes before four o'clock the other day and heard the steady ticking of that old clock. I listened as it sounded four times. I thought for a while about what I was hearing. That clock is well over a hundred years of age, and it is still faithfully ticking and sounding.

I cannot say how many moves I have left before my final

move. But I know I must emulate that clock. I must faithfully tick until my last moving day comes.

I know I cannot do this apart from the gracious help of the Lord. So these days I find myself saying:

> *Change and decay all around I see,*
> *O Thou who changest not, abide with me.*

(Henry F. Lyte)

-2-

From God's Word, the Bible...

The LORD is my light and my salvation;
Whom shall I fear?
The LORD is the strength of my life;
Of whom shall I be afraid?
Psalm 27:1

I sought the LORD, and He heard me,
And delivered me from all my fears.
Ps. 34:4.

In the multitude of my anxieties within me,
Your comforts delight my soul.
Psalm 94:19

Whenever I am Afraid

In Psalm 56:3, David admits to being afraid. To be afraid is to be "filled with fear or apprehension." That word "afraid" is all too familiar! We are often filled with fear and apprehension.

Most of our fears have to do with our lives or the lives of those we love either being lessened in quality or coming to an end.

Many things can lessen the quality of our lives or the lives of our loved ones—sickness, financial reversals, family discord, world conditions, and many other things. There is no shortage of things to bring about apprehension!

And the biggest one of all is death itself! How many people have proudly marched through life as if they were in control and as if they were sufficient for everything, only to tremble and cower when they came to death's door! Haughty and proud in his disdain for Christianity, skeptic David Hume whimpered at death: "I am affrighted and confounded with the forlorn solitude in which I am placed by my philosophy … I fancy myself in the most deplorable condition imaginable, environed in the deepest darkness."

The David who wrote Psalm 56:3 was the man who stood fearlessly before Goliath. But he was "very much afraid" when he took up his pen to write this psalm. He was in the land of the Philistines, where he did not belong, and it seemed to him that King Achish would soon snuff out his life (see 1 Sam. 21:12). But David collected himself, looked to God, and wrote: "Whenever I am afraid, I will trust in You."

"Whenever" means "at whatever time," or "at any or every time." In Psalm 56:3, it is a beautiful word! At whatever time or at any time David finds himself gripped with fear, he will trust in God. Every time he is afraid, he will trust God. Trusting is always the great antidote for fearing.

Are you, like David and so many others, frightened by the thought of death? Trust in God! He has both made glorious promises regarding death and has shown Himself to be utterly faithful to His promises.

What has God promised about this matter of death? He has promised His people will not face it alone, that He Himself will meet them in the "valley of the shadow" and will shepherd them safely through (Ps. 23:4). He has promised that at the very moment of death, the souls of His people will go immediately into His presence (2 Cor. 5:6-8). And He has promised that the bodies of all those who belong to Him will finally be raised from their graves, rejoined to their souls, and will forever be with Him in eternal glory (1 Thess. 4:13-18).

What promises! But please note that these are promises God has given only to His people! Not all are His people. Those who are not in a right relationship with Him have His promise that they will face Him in judgment and will be driven forever from His presence (2 Thess. 1:8-10). That will cause any thinking person to really be afraid! (Luke 12:4-5).

Are you afraid of that immensely sobering time when

you will have to stand before God in judgment? God has given a promise for you to trust. He has promised that He will forgive all those who trust completely in His Son, Jesus Christ, and in what He did on the cross for sinners like you and me (John 3:16,36; 5:24; 6:47; 1 John 5:11-12).

Those who believe in Jesus can rejoice in these words from the Apostle Paul: "There is therefore now no condemnation to those who are in Christ Jesus…" (Rom. 8:1).

Afraid? Don't be! Trust God's promise to save sinners and then trust His promises to take care of His people. Make it your policy to say to God: "Whenever I am afraid, I will trust in You."

-3-

From God's Word, the Bible...

And if you call on the Father, who without partiality judges according to each one's work, conduct yourselves throughout the time of your stay here in fear; knowing that you were not redeemed with corruptible things, like silver or gold, from your aimless conduct received by tradition from your fathers, but with the precious blood of Christ, as of a lamb without blemish and without spot. He indeed was foreordained before the foundation of the world, but was manifest in these last times for you.

1 Peter 1:17-20

"He, to Rescue Me from Danger, Interposed His Precious Blood"

Jesus sought me when a stranger,
Wandering from the fold of God;
He, to rescue me from danger,
Interposed His precious blood…

(*Come, Thou Fount of Every Blessing*,
Robert Robinson, 1758)

These words take us to the heart of Christ's saving work on behalf of His people. It was a matter of Jesus interposing His blood! That act of interposition makes His blood precious to every believer.

More about that in a moment! First, let's think about that word "danger." Frightening word! When we hear the word "danger," we tend to think of the people and the things that threaten our wellbeing and happiness in this world. There is no shortage of them.

There is, however, another type of danger which is much worse than any posed by this temporal realm. It is the danger of experiencing the wrath of God in eternity. People these days like to play down that danger, but no fair reading of the Bible will allow us to do so. All are agreed that the Old Testament places a heavy emphasis on the matter, but we must not think that the teaching of God's wrath is confined there. The same teaching is evenly distributed throughout the New Testament. It is in the Gospels (Matt. 3:12; 7:13-14; 22:13-14; 23:33; 25:30,41,46; Mark 9:42-29; Luke 16:19-31; John 3:36), in the epistles of Paul (Rom. 1:18-19; 2:5; 3:5; 4:15; 12:19; Eph. 2:3; 5:6), and in the other epistles as well (Heb. 10:27; 12:25-29; James 5:9; 1 Peter 4:17-18; 2 Peter 2:4-9).

It is the dominant theme of the book of Revelation (Rev. 6:16-17; 11:18; 14:10,19; 15:1,7; 16:1,19; 19:15; 20:11-15; 21:8; 22:11,15).

And for those who blissfully say: "Just give me the loving God of John 3:16," the wrath of God is powerfully present in the word "perish" which is mentioned in that very verse.

We will never understand Christianity until we realize that it is all about rescuing people from this danger! Jesus came to this world for the express purpose of dealing with that danger.

God is holy. He cannot merely ignore our sins as if they never happened. He has to pronounce a sentence on them and also has to carry out that sentence. What is His sentence on our sins? It is His wrath, which is eternal separation from Himself in hell.

The glory of Christianity is that Jesus on the cross took the wrath that we deserve for our sins. There He "interposed" or inserted His blood between the wrath of God and guilty sinners. The word "blood" means that He poured out His life in death. To say He interposed His blood is to say He interposed Himself. On the cross He took the position between the wrath of God and guilty sinners. The wrath fell on Him, and there is now no wrath left for all who repent of their sins and trust in Him. John 3:36 puts it perfectly: "He who believes in the Son has everlasting life; and he who does not believe the Son shall not see life, but the wrath of God abides on him."

But how could Jesus in the space of the six hours that He was on the cross (from 9:00 in the morning until 3:00 in the afternoon) receive an eternity's worth of the wrath of God for all sinners who believe in Him? The answer lies in the special nature of Jesus. He was no ordinary man. He was the God-man, fully God, fully man at one and the same time. As God, He was an infinite person, and as an infinite person, He could receive in a finite length of time an infinite measure of wrath. In other words, Jesus as an infinite person could receive in a finite measure of time what we as finite people would receive in an infinite measure of time.

When we truly understand what Jesus did on the cross for sinners, we gladly respond to Robert Robinson's phrase "precious blood" with a hearty "Yes!"

-4-

From God's Word, the Bible...

"Do you see this woman? I entered your house; you gave Me no water for My feet, but she has washed My feet with her tears and wiped them with the hair of her head. You gave Me no kiss, but this woman has not ceased to kiss My feet since the time I came in. You did not anoint My head with oil, but this woman has anointed My feet with fragrant oil. Therefore I say to you, her sins, which are many, are forgiven, for she loved much. But to whom little is forgiven, the same loves little."

Then He said to her, "Your sins are forgiven."

And those who sat at the table with Him began to say to themselves, "Who is this who even forgives sins?"

Then He said to the woman, "Your faith has saved you. Go in peace."

From Luke 7:36-50

Tell Me What You Think You Owe...

Tell me what you think you owe the Lord, and I will tell you how much you feel like serving Him. If you think you owe a great deal, you will gladly serve and worship Him. If you think you owe very little, you will not be much interested in service or worship.

The truth of the matter is every Christian owes the Lord the same amount. He has done no less for one than He has for others. We all come into this world in a very sad and sorrowful condition. We come in with a sinful nature that causes us to be alienated or separated from God.

The piercing question is this: How can sinful human beings ever hope to enjoy fellowship with the perfectly holy God? To put it another way, how can guilty sinners ever stand acceptably in the presence of the holy God?

The answer is that sin must be taken out of the way, and there is only one way that sin can be removed from between

God and us. Its penalty has to be paid! What is the penalty for sin? It is eternal separation from God or the eternal wrath of God!

There are only two ways for the penalty for our sins to be paid: we either have to pay it ourselves, which means we must be separated from God and heaven forever, or someone has to pay it on our behalf. In order for someone else to pay the penalty for our sins, such a person must, of course, be free from sin. We see the logic of this. If someone has sins of his own, he would have to pay the penalty for those and could not, therefore, pay the penalty for anyone else.

Jesus is the only person who ever lived without sin (John 1:14; 1 Peter 1:19; 1 John 3:5). Because He had no sins of His own, He could pay for the sins of others.

This is what His death on the cross is all about. There He received the wrath of God in the place of sinners. Because He was God in human flesh, He could receive in a finite length of time an infinite measure of wrath. This is the reason He cried out from the cross: "My God, My God, why have You forsaken Me?" (Matt. 27:46).

The cost of sin is God-forsakenness in hell, and, on that cross, Jesus endured God-forsakenness for sinners. All who realize the depth and guilt of their sins and entrust themselves fully to Jesus in the work He did on the cross are released from the sentence of God's wrath (John 3:16,36; Rom. 5:8-9;1 Thess. 1:10; 1 Peter 2:24).

What do Christians owe the Lord? A debt that can never be paid! We have been delivered from the wrath of God and given eternal life through Christ. In referring to a debt we owe, I am not suggesting that we must work for our salvation. Not for a moment! The Apostle Paul says: "For by grace you have been saved through faith, and that not of yourselves; it is the gift of God, not of works, lest anyone should boast" (Eph. 2:8-9).

We do not work *for* our salvation but *from* our salvation. Because we have been saved by the redeeming death of the Lord Jesus, we work to show our love and gratitude to Him.

It is not easy to show gratitude to the Lord by worshiping and serving Him. There are always a thousand things to occupy us. Some people excuse themselves from worship and service because they feel that they don't have the time. Other people do so because they have been offended or hurt. Yet others do so because they don't agree with the direction the church is going.

The answer to each of these excuses is the same: What do you owe? If you say that you owe nothing less than deliverance from the wrath of God to Christ, you must surely go on to say that He is worthy of your time and energy and that no hurt or disagreement is great enough to offset the debt.

What I have been saying is pointedly expressed in these words from Isaac Watts:

> *When I survey the wondrous cross*
> *On which the Prince of Glory died,*
> *My richest gain I count but loss,*
> *And pour contempt on all my pride.*
>
> *Forbid it, Lord, that I should boast,*
> *Save in the death of Christ my God;*
> *All the vain things that charm me most –*
> *I sacrifice them to His blood.*
>
> *Were the whole realm of nature mine,*
> *That were a present far too small:*
> *Love so amazing, so divine,*
> *Demands my soul, my life, my all.*

-5-

From God's Word, the Bible...

And as it is appointed for men to die once, but after this the judgment, so Christ was offered once to bear the sins of many. To those who eagerly wait for Him He will appear a second time, apart from sin, for salvation.

Hebrews 9:27-28

The Passing of a Celebrity

Michael Jackson is dead. At one time, he had great wealth. He still had great fame when he breathed his last. But now he is gone.

In reporting his death, one newsperson continued to express shock that this famous man had died at age fifty. It was as if he, the newsman, was assuming that one has to be a certain age to die!

But death is all around us all the time. We are reminded of it when we drive by a cemetery, hospital or nursing facility, or when we see an obituary column.

Death takes young and old, rich and poor, the well educated and the illiterate, conservative and liberal. The greatest fact of life is death. Martin Luther was right in saying the following words: "Life is a constant and daily journey toward death. One after another dies, and the living must merely engage in the miserable business of carrying one another to the grave. All of us are traveling the same road together."

The Bible tells us that the wise man thinks about what lies ahead and makes prudent preparation for it (Prov. 22:3). The fool never does.

If death is inevitable, is it not wise to think about it and prepare for it?

But how many there are who seem to think life is sure and death is uncertain. Just the opposite is true!

Many people, these days, would argue that there is nothing for which to prepare because death is the end. Really? Isn't there something inside you that screams that it is not so?

The Bible tells us that we were made *by* God and *for* God and we must meet God. It flatly says: "Prepare to meet your God…!" (Amos 4:12).

But how do we prepare for death? The Bible has the answer for that as well. It tells us to repent of our sins and to take the Lord Jesus Christ as our Savior. Why take Jesus? He has demonstrated His authority over death by rising from the grave.

If you don't know how to handle something, the best thing to do is go to someone who does know how to handle it. You and I are not able to handle death and what lies beyond it, but the Lord Jesus is able. If we place ourselves in His hands, we have nothing to fear about death or the hereafter.

But we must truly take Jesus as our Savior and not just go through the motions of doing so. If we really trust Him, it will show up in our lives. We will not try to govern our lives with no regard for Him, for His Book (the Bible), for His day (the Lord's Day), or for His church. Many who think they have received Christ have only deceived themselves.

I have come to love a song that urges people to come to

Jesus and "laugh on glory's side." There is indeed a glory side for those who receive Christ. It is called heaven. And Jesus is the way! If you want to take the fear out of death and "laugh on glory's side," turn to Christ now.

Because we never know when death will come, sooner is always better than later for fleeing to Christ.

-6-

From God's Word, the Bible...

Do not fear any of those things which you are about to suffer. Indeed, the devil is about to throw some of you into prison, that you may be tested, and you will have tribulation ten days. Be faithful until death, and I will give you the crown of life.

Revelation 2:10

Two Questions Most Church Attendees Dare Not Ask Themselves

Practically every church in my city of Jackson, Tennessee, cancelled services on May 2, 2010, because of the flood that brought about fifteen inches of rain to our area. My church was among those that canceled. So I sat at home that day and watched a lot of religious TV programming. As I viewed program after program, I was astonished at how little of the gospel I heard. Most of the messages focused on how to make life in this world more enjoyable and comfortable. It was much like watching Oprah or Dr. Phil!

I admit that the Bible does say a good bit about living in this world, but it is always does so in connection with the gospel and as a consequence of the gospel. It was a clear statement of the gospel that was so noticeably missing in most of the programs I viewed. So I found myself thinking about two questions that most church attendees dare not ask themselves. The first is this: Is what I am getting from my church real Christianity? Christianity is not just a successful living technique. It is the declaration of what God has done in and through Jesus to rescue sinners from their sins and the wrath to come and to give them right standing with God and eternal glory.

There is no Christianity without the gospel, and if you are in a church that doesn't emphasize the gospel, you are not really in a church at all.

That led me to a second question: If I am not getting real Christianity from my church, why am I supporting it?

Some would say it is because there is so much "energy" in the services. However, the prophets of Baal had lots and lots of energy, and they were horribly wrong (1 Kings 18:25-28).

Some would say it is because the church offers so many activities for the children. The Bible says parents are to bring their children up in the teaching of the Lord! No parent can discharge this responsibility if he has his children in a church that does not preach the gospel.

Some would say it is because the crowd is so large. But the Bible tells us not to follow a crowd to do evil (Exod. 23:2).

On the rainy day as I sat at home, I also found myself thinking about another day—the day of God's judgment. How sad it will be for many so-called Christian pastors to stand in the presence of the Lord and be faced with the enormous realization that they had never really preached Christianity at all! (1 Cor. 3:10-17). And how very sad it will be on that day for the multitudes of professing Christians to realize that they had spent most of their lives going to churches where they never really heard the Christian message at all!

If you had asked me on that day if we needed the flood, I would have said: "No way!"

But if you were to ask me today if I can think of a flood that we do need, I would answer with an emphatic yes. We need a spiritual flood, the flood depicted in these words:

> *Rain down, you heavens, from above,*
> *And let the skies pour down righteousness;*
> *Let the earth open, let them bring forth salvation,*
> *And let righteousness spring up together.*
> (Isa. 45:8)

Such a flood would sweep away that which is false and flimsy, and restore the gospel to the priority it deserves.

-7-

From God's Word, the Bible...

God forbid that I should boast except in the cross of our Lord Jesus Christ, by whom the world has been crucified to me, and I to the world.

Galatians 6:14

Christianity or "Ianity"?

The Apostle Paul was not in doubt about what he should preach. He put it very clearly: "I determined not to know anything among you except Jesus Christ and Him crucified" (1 Cor. 2:2).

It's obvious that Paul was a preacher of Christianity. The word "Christianity" has Christ in it, and Paul preached Christ.

Many preachers these days cannot echo the words of Paul. They are not preachers of Christ, and if we take Christ out of Christianity, we have something called "Ianity."

Isn't it interesting that "Ianity" begins with "I"? Much of what we call Christianity these days has very little to do with Christ and a lot to do with us. Our worship is not about Christ and His great deeds. It is about us and how we feel about things. And our great concern is not serving God. It is rather getting God to serve us. We don't want to fall before Him as our Sovereign. We want Him to be our helper with all the little aggravations and challenges that life brings our way. These are the days of the "troubleshooter" God. We don't want much to do with Him, but we want Him to be ready to spring into action if we need Him!

Maybe He can keep our children from spilling their milk or keep the dog from coming into the house with muddy feet!

We don't want a God who talks about sin. That would make us feel bad! And we aren't all that interested in heaven. We want our best life now!

The thing we so often fail to see is that the smaller we make God, the more unnecessary we make Him! Many these days are starved for the greatness of God. If they were to speak to our churches, they might very well say: "We will take care of the milk and the dog; give us a God that can do for us what we cannot do for ourselves."

What is it we cannot do for ourselves? We can't rid ourselves of sin, lift from ourselves the sentence of God's condemnation, or prepare ourselves to stand acceptably in the presence of a holy God. But through the Lord Jesus Christ, God forgives sinners, cancels the sentence of condemnation, and declares those sinners to be guiltless. While so many pursue the God who specializes in trivia, the Bible calls us to pursue the God who specializes in salvation. This is Christianity!

Some time ago, Michael Horton, a professor in California, wrote a book entitled *Christless Christianity*. Some undoubtedly responded to that title by saying: "That's nonsense. You can't have Christianity with Christ!" And that is the sharp point of the book! When you take Christ out of Christianity, you have something, but it is no longer Christianity. Let's just call it "Ianity," which, by the way, is only one letter, the letter "n," away from "inanity," that is "a lack of substance" or "shallowness."

There you have it! Christianity without Christ is shallow and empty.

While it professes to be profound, it is far from it.

There are two things that every true believer in Christ should dread above everything else. One is a Christless Bible and the other is a crossless Christ. "Ianity" offers us both! It takes Christ out of the Bible and makes it some sort of miscellaneous collection of tips and guidelines for living better, and when "Ianity" does give us one of its infrequent mentions of Christ, it is not the Christ who endured the wrath of God on the cross for sinners. It is, rather, the Christ who helps us implement the tips! Christianity, on the other hand, rightly sees Christ as the subject of the whole Bible (Luke 24:27,44) and rightly emphasizes that Christ came to this earth to die on that cross, and that there is no hope for salvation except in that redeeming death.

-8-

From God's Word, the Bible...

Do not fret because of evildoers,
Nor be envious of the workers of iniquity.
For they shall soon be cut down like the grass,
And wither as the green herb.
Trust in the LORD, and do good;
Dwell in the land, and feed on His faithfulness.
Delight yourself also in the LORD,
And He shall give you the desires of your heart.

From Psalm 37:1-11

The Danger of Snapshot Theology

The Christian life is not easy! Anyone who tells you that it is, doesn't know what he's talking about. The Lord Jesus tells us that following Him means denying ourselves and carrying a cross (Matt. 16:24). The Apostle Paul tells us that the Christian life is a warfare (Eph. 6:10-20).

Sometimes, however, we make the Christian life harder than it needs to be. Living for the Lord is much easier when we trust the Lord to always have our best interests at heart and to always be with us in every difficult circumstance. It becomes immensely more difficult when we doubt these things.

Sadly enough, many Christians do doubt that God really cares for them. They are disappointed with Him. He has not lived up to their expectations.

One thing that inevitably leads to disappointment with

God is what I call "snapshot theology." What is snapshot theology? It is drawing conclusions about God on the basis of the circumstances in which we find ourselves at this moment.

How easy it is to do this! We often find that our circumstances are a lot less desirable than we would have them to be, and on the basis of those circumstances we conclude that God has failed us. We can be sure that the devil is ever eager to help us draw that conclusion. He is very quick to speak along these lines: "If God truly loved you, you wouldn't have these problems."

I have often said that if we begin with the wrong job description for God, He will always fail in our eyes. If we assume that it is God's job to make life as comfortable for us as it can possibly be, we are bound to think ill of Him when our lives are not comfortable. But the problem is not with God; it is rather with our wrong thinking about Him. God has never told us that His purpose is to make life easy for us.

What is His purpose? It is to conform us to the image of His Son (Rom. 8:29). In other words, it is to bring us to spiritual maturity.

Thank God, the trials of this life will someday come to an end. The tide of time will wash up on the shore of eternity. There, in the glory of God's presence, we will have a new and different perspective on the problems of this life. There we will not simply look at one snapshot from our lives, but God will rather show us the whole movie. As we are made aware of all that God was accomplishing in our lives, we will certainly find that our disappointment with Him has vanished and we will be lost in "wonder, love and praise."

It may be hard for us to believe now, but the truth of the matter is this: when God's people get home to glory and there see how He worked in their lives, their testimony will be: "He has done all things well."

The business before us is to simply trust even when we do not understand. We must trust God's *heart* even when we cannot trace His *hand*. No Christian should ever be in doubt about the heart of God. He put it clearly on display when He nailed His Son to the cross to die for our sins. As hard as it is to believe, the fact is our difficult circumstances do not mean God's heart has changed. Those difficulties come from that same heart of love.

-9-

From God's Word, the Bible...

Then the angel said to them, "Do not be afraid, for behold, I bring you good tidings of great joy which will be to all people. For there is born to you this day in the city of David a Savior, who is Christ the Lord. And this will be the sign to you: You will find a Babe wrapped in swaddling cloths, lying in a manger."
And suddenly there was with the angel a multitude of the heavenly host praising God and saying:
"Glory to God in the highest,
And on earth peace, goodwill toward men!"

From Luke 2:8-14

Cookie the Christmas Dog and the Repackaging of Christmas

Years ago, Sylvia and I had a dog named Cookie. She was a delight. I still miss her. Cookie was our Christmas dog and she loved Christmas.

One year Sylvia and I returned home to find that Cookie had opened some of the Christmas presents! Suffice it to say, it was necessary for us to do some repackaging.

But there is some Christmas re-packaging these days that is not necessary. Let me explain.

Most church leaders want to see their churches grow in membership and in attendance. I say "most" because I have met a few folks down through the years who preferred for the church to stay small. In one of my previous pastorates, a deacon got upset because our church was growing so much! Imagine that! I think he had a Diotrephes problem (see 3 John 9).

The other extreme consists of those who are willing to do anything to see their churches grow. This is the explanation for much of modern-day Christendom, which is in the grip of what may be called a sinister sequence.

This sequence begins with church leaders asking this question: "What can we do to get our church to grow?"

The answer to that question often amounts to this: We must get people to like us! The reasoning here is that if people like us, they will want to be around us, and if they want to be around us, they will come to church.

That, of course, leads to yet another question: What can we do to get people to like us?

And the answer to that is often along these lines: We must give them what they want and stop giving them things they don't want.

It doesn't take a lot of research to determine that people these days don't want to hear about sin, judgment to come or a man dying on a cross. So we must get rid of these things! Out with them! We must not allow ourselves to be troubled by the fact that for centuries these very things were considered to be the essential, non-negotiable core of Christianity! We must repackage Christianity into something that is marketable today!

When the repackaging is done, we have a Christianity that is more like a successful-living philosophy. We tell people to believe in Jesus so they can be happy in this life. The one fact that the re-packagers seem to be unwilling to face is this: there are plenty of non-Christians who are very happy with their lives! So when we tell them to accept Jesus to be happy, they simply smile and say, "No, thank you. We're already quite happy without Jesus. You may need Him, but we don't. So keep Him to yourself."

The truth of the matter is that many people today are presenting the Christian message in such a way that they are giving others a perfectly good reason for rejecting it.

But do we not run into the same problem when we tell people that they need Jesus because they are sinners? Can they not merely say that they don't feel like they are sinners and, therefore, do not need Jesus? Yes, they can say it, but the evidence is against them, and the voice of conscience tells them that the evidence is against them!

The church today finds herself in the peculiar position of telling people they need Jesus as their Savior after she, the church, has removed from her teaching any reason for people to need a Savior.

When we next approach the Christmas season, we would do well to reflect deeply on the words the angel spoke to Joseph: "… you shall call His name JESUS, for He will save His people from their sins" (Matt. 1:21).

Only sinners need saving. Since we are all sinners (Rom. 3:23), we all need saving. The good news of Christmas is that the Savior has come into the world. His name is Jesus. And He will save all those who see the reality and enormity of their sins and come to Him for saving.

-10-

From God's Word, the Bible...

For He made Him who knew no sin to be sin for us, that we might become the righteousness of God in Him.

2 Corinthians 5:21

And the Award for "Best-Dressed" Goes to...

Part of the silliness that surrounds the Oscar Awards each year is the prolonged discussion about the way in which the actors and actresses are dressed.

I recently came across this discussion on the TV Guide Channel. I was checking the listings, and there it was—two men and two women discussing, for the most part, the way in which the actresses were dressed. I didn't stay watching it for long, but it did get me to thinking again about the shallowness of this age.

It also got me to thinking again about how people are so absorbed with things that are passing that they give absolutely no thought to those things that last.

Take this matter of dress, for instance. The Bible teaches

us that we must all leave this world and stand before God. It tells us that before we can enter into heaven we must be dressed in perfect righteousness.

It further tells us that we do not possess this righteousness ourselves. Because of our sinfulness, we are clothed in filthy rags.

But the good news of the Bible is this: we do not have to stand before the holy God in our filthy rags. By His righteous living, the Lord Jesus provided the garment that God demands. That garment of perfect righteousness can and will be ours if, while we are still in this life, we come to God and ask Him to grant us the perfect righteousness of Christ.

Eternal dress is far more important than temporal dress, but how very, very many people there are who concern themselves exclusively with the latter. They remind me of the Roman soldiers at the crucifixion of Jesus who gambled for His garments. Shockingly, they were gambling for temporal garments while being completely oblivious to the garment of salvation that Jesus was providing on that cross.

Those who go all through life thinking only about temporal things are in for a rude awakening. This is pictured for us in Matthew 22:1-14 which tells us that there will come a day when those who are not clothed in the perfect righteousness of Christ will be discovered and cast out of God's kingdom forever. May God help you to see the importance of receiving the righteousness of Christ.

As I listened to the boring discussion about the best-dressed actresses, I could not help but say: "The award for best-dressed goes to … Christians." They are dressed in the righteousness of Christ. Their award is heaven itself.

I hope these lines make you stop and think about how you appear—and not how you appear to your friends but how you appear to God. It is also a good idea for you to begin thinking about how you will be clothed when you stand before God in judgment.

Those who, by faith, are clothed in the righteousness of Christ take as their own these words:

> *I will greatly rejoice in the Lord,*
> *My soul shall be joyful in my God;*
> *For He has clothed me with the garments of salvation,*
> *He has covered me with the robe of righteousness,*
> *As a bridegroom decks himself with ornaments,*
> *And as a bride adorns herself with her jewels.*

(Isa. 61:10)

-11-

From God's Word, the Bible...

Behold, I tell you a mystery: We shall not all sleep, but we shall all be changed—in a moment, in the twinkling of an eye, at the last trumpet. For the trumpet will sound, and the dead will be raised incorruptible, and we shall be changed. For this corruptible must put on incorruption, and this mortal must put on immortality. So when this corruptible has put on incorruption, and this mortal has put on immortality, then shall be brought to pass the saying that is written: "Death is swallowed up in victory."

From 1 Corinthians 15:50-58

Vacationing in a Cemetery

In the fall some years ago, my wife and I did something we had dreamed about for years: we took in the beauty of the northeast. We enjoyed seeing Niagara Falls and the breathtaking foliage of New York, New Hampshire, and Vermont. We also enjoyed visiting the church in Northampton, Massachusetts, where the great theologian Jonathan Edwards served as pastor.

Oddly enough, the highlight of the trip for me was a cemetery in Arlington, Vermont, where we had journeyed to see the Norman Rockwell museum.

The cemetery was very old, with some graves dating back to the late 1700s. One of the gravestones immediately caught my attention. It marked the resting place of a Daniel Ellsworth, who died February 25, 1832, at the age of fifty. I was glad to read these words on the marker:

Thus saith the Comforter,
Earth has no sorrows
Which Heaven cannot heal.

Another stone marked the grave of Samuel Ellsworth, who died July 18, 1819, at the age of 65. At the bottom of this marker was this verse of Scripture: "And what I say unto you I say unto all, 'Watch'." (Mark 13:37).

As we toured the cemetery, we found that almost every gravestone had words expressing faith in Christ. The inscription I liked best was at the grave of Captain John Gray, who died at age seventy-nine in 1806:

When Christ appears in yonder Cloud
With all His numerous Throng
This believer then shall rise & sing
And Christ shall be the song.

Still another stone was inscribed with these words:

Friends nor Physicians could not save
My mortal body from the grave;
Nor can the grave confine me here,
When Christ my Savior shall appear.

As I walked away from that cemetery, the words of Hebrews 11:4 came to mind: " … he being dead still speaks."

The believers whose graves I visited are still speaking hundreds of years after they died. They must have died with the realization that their gravestones would be read by hundreds and thousands from future generations. They wanted even in death to speak plainly to the living about the brevity of life, the certainty of death, and the urgent need to prepare to meet God. They also wanted to bear witness to the only way to stand acceptably in the presence of God, namely, through faith in the saving work of the Lord Jesus Christ.

Still further, they intended in death to taunt death. Even though death had claimed them, it would not be able to hold them. They went to their graves with the unswerving confidence that the very Christ in whom they trusted would come again from heaven, call their bodies from those graves, reunite those bodies to their souls (which went to be with the Lord at the time of death—2 Cor. 5:8), and personally escort them to share in His eternal glory.

I left that cemetery with gratitude swelling up in my heart for the strong and unwavering testimony of those saints of God. I also left praying that unbelievers who visit there would realize the brevity of this life, the certainty of eternity, and the sufficiency of Jesus Christ to prepare them for eternity.

-12-

From God's Word, the Bible...

"Beware of false prophets, who come to you in sheep's clothing, but inwardly they are ravenous wolves. You will know them by their fruits. Do men gather grapes from thornbushes or figs from thistles? Even so, every good tree bears good fruit, but a bad tree bears bad fruit. A good tree cannot bear bad fruit, nor can a bad tree bear good fruit. Every tree that does not bear good fruit is cut down and thrown into the fire. Therefore by their fruits you will know them.

Matthew 7:15-20

Who Is Really Relevant?

Scarcely a week can go by without a piece of mail coming my way about a new church starting up—at least that is the way it seems. It won't be long until there are more churches in my city than there are people to attend them!

These pieces of mail almost invariably promise that the new church will be "relevant," "contemporary," "practical," and "uplifting."

There is no great secret here. The churches that use these words are telling us that they will be offering a message about how to live happily and successfully in this world. They are telling us that they will give people help with their finances, their careers, their families, and their personal relationships. They are telling us that we can come to their services without having to fear that we will hear such words as "sin," "judgment," and "repentance." Those words make people feel bad, and these churches want people to feel good! Still further, these pastors and churches are telling us how they regard pastors and churches that still use such words. They are irrelevant, they say!

So I have been thinking about who is relevant and who isn't. Here is a man who has a dreadful and serious illness. He goes to Doctor A, and this doctor tells him that there is nothing seriously wrong with him, and that he simply needs to have a more positive outlook on life. But our patient has the gnawing sense that something is wrong. So he goes to Doctor B. This doctor runs certain tests. On the basis of those tests he tells this man that he, the doctor, has both bad news and good news. The bad news is that he, the patient, has an illness that is so serious that it will eventually kill him; but the good news is that the illness can be successfully treated.

Which of the two doctors is more relevant for this poor man? Now Doctor A may be a very likable, warm, and personable fellow. He may be very witty, clever, and entertaining. He may even give the man tips on how to handle his finances and career and so on. But he is certainly not relevant because he refuses to take seriously the terrible illness that his patient has. Doctor A may consider himself relevant, but in reality he is horribly irrelevant!

Doctor B, on the other hand, may be somewhat lacking in personal charm. He may not be funny or entertaining at all. He may not have any tips for his patient with regard to other areas of his life. He may even dress in a traditional rather than trendy way! But he is powerfully relevant because he acknowledges the illness of his patient and he treats it!

Like it or not, the Bible is very plain about us. It tells us that we are sinful people who are destined to stand at the Judgment Seat of the God who is infinitely holy.

This life will soon pass, and each one of us will face the awesome realities of judgment and eternity. Pastors and churches are called by God to be physicians of souls. We are called to tell people about the reality of their sin and the certainty of divine judgment and also, thank God, to tell them that there is a cure for sin. If they will flee to the Lord Jesus Christ in true repentance and faith, they can be saved!

So who really is relevant? Is it the pastor who refuses to tell people about their sin and the salvation available in Christ? Or is it the pastor who does? The answer is plain. It is one of the great ironies of our time that many pastors who seem to be relevant are really irrelevant, and many pastors who seem to be irrelevant are relevant!

In these days in which preachers are falling all over themselves to help people live in the here and now, we would do well to ever heed these words from the Lord Jesus Christ: "Do not labor for the food which perishes, but for the food which endures to everlasting life, which the Son of Man will give you, because God the Father has set His seal on Him" (John 6:27).

We would also do well to reflect long and hard on the Bible's warnings to not heal the hurt of people "slightly" and not preach peace when there is no peace (Jer. 6:14; 8:11).

-13-

From God's Word, the Bible...

And Jehoiada the priest gave to the captains of hundreds the spears and the large and small shields which had belonged to King David, that were in the temple of God. Then he set all the people, every man with his weapon in his hand, from the right side of the temple to the left side of the temple, along by the altar and by the temple, all around the king. And they brought out the king's son, put the crown on him, gave him the Testimony, and made him king. Then Jehoiada and his sons anointed him, and said,
"Long live the king!"

From 2 Chronicles 23:1-11

The Epitaph Every Christian Should Desire

Mel Blanc's gravestone has these words: "That's all folks." Merv Griffin's reads: "I will not be right back after this message."

A lesser-known epitaph is found on the gravestone of one Lester Moore:

> *Here lies Lester Moore,*
> *Four slugs from a 44.*
> *No less, no more.*

Epitaphs don't have to be written on tombstones. They can be any phrase or statement written or spoken in memory of a person who has died.

It is inevitable that others will have something to say about us when we die. Perhaps they will say: "He was a good family man," or "She was a good wife and mother." Perhaps someone will say: "He had a great sense of humor."

What people say of us after we have died will be determined by how we live. Each one of us is now writing a script that will be read when we die. Every Christian should be trying to live in such a way that others, upon his or her death, will have to say the very same thing that the author of 2 Chronicles said of Jehoiada: he (or she) did good "toward God and His house."

Jehoiada is not one of the best-known characters of the Old Testament. That is a shame. He was a great man indeed. When Queen Athaliah was working feverishly to obliterate all the descendants of David, Jehoiada and his wife hid the infant Joash until he was old enough to serve as king At that time Jehoiada put together a plan to put Joash on the throne. It was a plan that worked perfectly. So Jehoiada stood for God in a very evil time and when there were many who stood against God. Jehoiada also believed God's Word even when it seemed absurd to do so. God had promised that David's line would last. With that line down to a single child, there seemed to be little chance of that promise being fulfilled. But Jehoiada continued to believe in that promise, and he believed that God could use him to make the fulfillment a reality.

Jehoiada is still doing good. He rises from the pages of Scripture to urge us to stand for God and to believe His Word. Even in difficult times? Yes!

We should be like Jehoiada. We should earnestly desire to do good toward God for one simple reason: He has done good toward us! If we only had adequate discernment, we could each list a thousand good things that we have received from God. All Christians would put at the top of that list the greatest of all good things—the good thing God did for us when He saved us from our sins and from the eternal destruction those sins deserve.

The way God did this good thing for us was, of course, through the redeeming work of His Son, the Lord Jesus Christ. Perhaps the greatest good we can get from Jehoiada the priest is to look past him to a greater priest who did greater good. That priest is Jesus; that good is salvation for sinners.

We should also fervently desire to do good toward God's house for the same reason—it has done good for us. How often we have come to it with weary, aching hearts only to find that the Lord met us there, opened His Word to us, and encouraged us!

We owe both God and His house a debt that we can never pay, but we can be making payments! We can live for God. We can always speak His name with reverence. We can obey His commandments. We can seek Him in prayer. We can exalt Him in worship. We can be faithful to attend church. We can protect the unity of the church. We can support the mission of the church. And we can pray for the success of the church. While others only live to do good for themselves, let us determine that we will be Jehoiadas who do good toward God and His church.

-14-

From God's Word, the Bible...

I have rejoiced in the way of Your testimonies,
As much as in all riches.
I will meditate on Your precepts,
And contemplate Your ways.
I will delight myself in Your statutes;
I will not forget Your word.

Your testimonies are wonderful;
Therefore my soul keeps them.
The entrance of Your words gives light;
It gives understanding to the simple.
I opened my mouth and panted,
For I longed for Your commandments.

Psalm 119:14-16; 129-131

A Little Skimping

Years ago I saw an amusing yet thought-provoking cartoon depicting two stone masons with trowels in hand walking away from a sign that read "Future site of the Tower of Pisa." One of them was saying: "I skimped a little on the foundation, but no one will ever know the difference."

A little skimping here and there can make a huge difference.

Just as we receive physical life through physical birth so we receive spiritual life through spiritual birth (John 1:12-13; 3:1-8).

Babies are adorable, but parents do not want their children to remain babies. They want them to grow. So it is in the spiritual realm. We come into it as spiritual babies, but God doesn't want us to remain babies. He wants us to grow.

The Word of God is the primary means that God has appointed for our spiritual growth. It is to us, spiritually, what food is to us, physically. The Apostle Peter urged his readers to "desire the pure milk of the word" so that they could "grow thereby" (1 Peter 2:2).

Nothing is more important to our spiritual health than the intake of the Word of God. We are to do this privately by reading it, studying it, reading about it, discussing it, and reflecting on it. And we are to do it publicly. We are to gather with our brothers and sisters in Christ in a church that accurately preaches and teaches the Word of God. As it is preached and taught, we are to give our full attention to it. J.I. Packer was right to make this point:

> *Congregations never honor God more than by reverently listening to His Word…*

But what if we begin to "skimp a little"? Yes, what then? What if we decide to cut back in our worship attendance? We may think that it will not hurt us spiritually, but sustained absence from God's Word will prove detrimental to our spiritual health, just as sustained absence from eating will prove detrimental to our physical health.

Sadly enough, churches and pastors are promoting the skimping mentality by greatly reducing the number of opportunities for people to hear the preaching of God's Word. My wife and I grew up in an era in which there were a great many opportunities to hear God's Word. There was preaching on Sunday morning and Sunday evening and teaching in a midweek service (and these services were never cancelled during holidays). And our country churches had "revival services." These were two-week events that were conducted in the spring and the fall, and, yes, there was preaching every night. We (my wife and I) estimate that, barring illness, we were in a hundred-and-fifty preaching services a year. Many churches these days would be challenged to offer fifty such services. Is this skimping hurting us? I believe it is. We are living in very dark and critical times. We need answers. The Bible alone contains the answers we need. It tells us why we are the way we are and what God has done in and through His Son, Jesus Christ, to change us. We need more of the Bible, not less. We need it in large doses, and it is hard to get those doses in this era of skimping.

-15-

From God's Word, the Bible...

And when Jesus was in Bethany at the house of Simon the leper, a woman came to Him having an alabaster flask of very costly fragrant oil, and she poured it on His head as He sat at the table. But when His disciples saw it, they were indignant, saying, "Why this waste? For this fragrant oil might have been sold for much and given to the poor."

But when Jesus was aware of it, He said to them, "Why do you trouble the woman? For she has done a good work for Me. For you have the poor with you always, but Me you do not have always.

For in pouring this fragrant oil on My body, she did it for My burial. Assuredly, I say to you, wherever this gospel is preached in the whole world, what this woman has done will also be told as a memorial to her."

Matthew 26:6-13

Why This Waste?

The disciples could scarcely believe their eyes. While they and Jesus were enjoying supper at the house of Simon the leper (evidently this was Simon's expression of gratitude to Jesus for healing him of his leprosy), a woman came to Jesus, broke open a box of very costly oil, and poured it out on His head.

Filled with indignation, the disciples pounced on the poor woman. "Why this waste?" was their stern question (Matt. 26:8).

This was foolish, extravagant, and senseless, they inferred. The poor could have certainly used the money that would have been realized had the ointment been sold. What this woman had done was, therefore, tantamount to taking food out of the mouths of the poor.

This outburst represented an aberration for the disciples. They certainly did not believe that anything done for Jesus would be a waste. But there are those who do so believe. What was a momentary glitch for the disciples is a settled mentality with many people these days. They look at the church and pronounce it all a waste—a waste of time, energy, and money. To them it is all so foolish and senseless. Those who give themselves to the Lord's work are frequently considered to be rather pathetic souls who could, were it not for their lack of enlightenment, be giving themselves to things that really matter. When they see Christians doing anything in the name of Christ, they eagerly resurrect the disciples' question: "Why this waste?"

These critics would have said the same when some of David's men did an extraordinary thing to get David a drink from Bethlehem's well. You remember the story. David was a fugitive, hiding in the cave of Adullam from the murderous rage of King Saul. And Bethlehem, his beloved home, was now in the hands of the Philistines.

Difficulties and hardships have a way of making us yearn for easier, simpler times. We are not surprised, then, that there in the cave David was thinking about his childhood years.

One of the pleasures of summertime was coming to Bethlehem while bathed in sweat and covered in grime and drawing a cool, refreshing drink from the well at the gate.

As David pondered that happier time, these words suddenly slipped out: "Oh, that someone would give me a drink of water from the well of Bethlehem, which is by the gate" (2 Sam. 23:15).

Caught up in that moment of nostalgia, David may very well not have even heard himself say those words. But others heard him. Three of his "mighty men" took the bare expression of that wish so very seriously that they broke through the Philistine lines, drew water from the well of Bethlehem, and brought it to David (2 Sam. 23:16).

What drove these men to do this? It was love for their captain, love so deep and strong that they regarded his mere wish as their duty, and, yes, their highest privilege. Some would call what they did foolhardy, but it made perfect sense to David's men. They loved their captain so much that they were willing to "waste" time and energy to please him.

And it was love for the Lord Jesus that drove Mary to "waste" her ointment. She had been enabled to foresee Jesus' saving work on the cross. The disciples had undoubtedly congratulated themselves on being terribly perceptive about her act, but this woman they belittled far outpaced them in perception. Her anointing of Jesus flowed from nothing less than a heart amazed at the thought of Calvary's love.

> *She looked down the corridor of days*
> *Saw Calvary's love and stood amazed.*
> *She saw that dying form, that disfigured face,*
> *And marveled at the sight of redeeming grace.*

Those who understand the cross of Christ and marvel at God's redeeming grace are ready to respond to the skeptics. With hearts full of love, we emphatically say: It is no waste to pour out the ointment of our lives in the worship and service of Jesus Christ. Through Him we have been rescued from condemnation and made heirs of eternal life. He is our glorious Savior. It is not a waste to serve Him. It is rather a waste not to serve Him. Going back to David's men for a moment, we must say that Christ, the captain of our salvation (Heb. 2:10), is far greater than David ever was. He is worthy of greater devotion than David's men showed him.

-16-

From God's Word, the Bible...

Then one of the criminals who were hanged blasphemed Him, saying, "If You are the Christ, save Yourself and us." But the other, answering, rebuked him, saying, "Do you not even fear God, seeing you are under the same condemnation? And we indeed justly, for we receive the due reward of our deeds; but this Man has done nothing wrong." Then he said to Jesus, "Lord, remember me when You come into Your kingdom."

And Jesus said to him, "Assuredly, I say to you, today you will be with Me in Paradise."

Luke 23:39-43

The Dying Thief Rejoiced to See That Fountain in His Day

There is a fountain filled with blood,
Drawn from Immanuel's veins,
And sinners plunged beneath that flood
Lose all their guilty stains.

The dying thief rejoiced to see
That fountain in His day;
And there may I, though vile as he,
Wash all my sins away.

(*There is a Fountain*, William Cowper, 1772)

One of the greatest joys of heaven will be meeting all the interesting people who will be there. I am looking forward to meeting the thief to whom William Cowper referred when he wrote these words.

This is the thief of Luke 23:39-43. It is the thief who, after initially heaping scorn and mockery on Jesus, cried to Him: "Lord remember me when you come into Your kingdom."

It is the thief who heard these enormously cheering words from Jesus: "Today you will be with Me in paradise."

But doesn't a "fountain filled with blood" sound strange? Cowper chose his words carefully, basing them squarely on this promise: "In that day a fountain shall be opened for the house of David and for the inhabitants of Jerusalem, for sin and for uncleanness" (Zech. 13:1). We know a fountain is a device that sends out a stream of water. We associate it with a constant and abundant supply of water. Cowper was affirming that Jesus' death on the cross opened a constant and abundant supply of cleansing for sinners.

How does the blood of Jesus cleanse sinners? The blood is shorthand for the death of the Lord Jesus, and death in all its forms (physical, spiritual, eternal) is the penalty for sin. On the cross Jesus took that penalty so all who trust in Him will never have to bear it themselves.

The thief "rejoiced" to see that fountain. He was about to go out into eternity laden down with his many violations of God's laws. His case would seem to be hopeless. But the grace of God enabled him to understand that the man next to him was no ordinary man dying an ordinary death. He was there as the King of an eternal kingdom, and He was dying so that even the vilest of sinners could be part of that kingdom. All that was necessary was for this thief to cry out to this King, and cry he did.

The fountain He opened on the cross is still flowing. It cleanses all sinners who cry out to Christ in repentance and faith. Even great sinners? Yes, even great sinners!

John Newton certainly fell into the category of a great sinner. Slave trader, drunkard, brawler, blasphemer—Newton was all that and more. But he found the Lord, or, more accurately, the Lord found him. Are you thinking that the name John Newton sounds familiar? It should. He is the author of the much-loved and much-sung *Amazing Grace*:

> *Amazing grace! how sweet the sound,*
> *That saved a wretch like me!*
> *I once was lost, but now am found,*
> *Was blind, but now I see.*

When Newton lay dying his friend John Jay came to visit him. Jay leaned over him and asked: "John, do you know me?" Newton replied: "I only know two things. I am a great sinner, and Jesus is a great Savior."

One of the most beautiful sights of heaven will be seeing the repentant thief standing alongside Newton—both great sinners, both saved by grace. We may even hear the thief say to Newton: "John, let's sing that song you wrote once again." If I do happen to hear him say that, I will gladly join in, singing most heartily:

> *How precious did that grace appear*
> *The hour I first believed!*

But the truth of the matter is that we are all great sinners. Paul writes: "There is none righteous, no, not one" (Rom. 3:10). So we all need to turn to Christ as this thief did.

While we rejoice over the conversion of this thief, we should never forget that there was another thief who did not repent. It was not mere coincidence that Jesus' cross was placed between the crosses of the two thieves. He is ever the great divider of men. Those who receive Him are saved; those who reject Him are forever lost. Nothing is of greater importance than making sure we are in the company of the believing thief and not in the company of the other.

-17-

From God's Word, the Bible...

"Therefore whoever hears these sayings of Mine, and does them, I will liken him to a wise man who built his house on the rock: and the rain descended, the floods came, and the winds blew and beat on that house; and it did not fall, for it was founded on the rock. … But everyone who hears these sayings of Mine, and does not do them, will be like a foolish man who built his house on the sand: and the rain descended, the floods came, and the winds blew and beat on that house; and it fell. And great was its fall."

From Matthew 7:21-29

Why Does Christianity Seem to Mean so Little to so Many?

Having served as a pastor for many years, I have come to this disconcerting conclusion: Christianity doesn't mean much to a lot of people who regard themselves as Christians.

Christians believe that they have been delivered from God's just punishment for their sins—eternal destruction in hell—because Jesus Christ endured their hell when He died on the cross. By virtue of the Spirit of God operating in their hearts, Christians have repented of their sins and put their trust for eternal salvation in the Lord Jesus and in what He did on their behalf.

There is nothing we can do to earn our salvation, but there are many things we can do to show our gratitude for salvation. Here are a few:

- We can read and study God's Word to discover how He wants us to live, and then live according to the things we discover.
- We can talk to the Lord in prayer, personally expressing to Him our gratitude for what He has done for us and asking Him to help us live for Him.
- We can worship Him in His house on a weekly basis (which, by the way, is one of His commandments).
- We can generously give money to support the Lord's work. Tithing is a good place to start!
- We can show love and appreciation to those whom God has sent to help us live for Him. (And, yes, I'm referring to pastors!)

These and the other things that God requires of us would seem to be the very least Christians can do to express their gratitude to God for graciously delivering them from hell. One would think every Christian would gladly do all that God asks and then say: "What more can I do?" After all, being delivered from hell is no small thing!

But, amazingly enough, many people who profess to be Christians find these things to be too much for them. They never read their Bibles or pray. They never, or very rarely, attend church services. They give little or nothing to the Lord's work. They do not pray for their pastors or come to hear their preaching and teaching. They say they are Christians, but they feel no gratitude. They say they are saved, but they do not feel indebted. They say their hell has been replaced with heaven, but they do not feel obligated to do anything for God.

So church leaders find themselves confronted with this question: Why does Christianity seem to mean very little or nothing to these people who claim to be Christians?

There are two answers. The first is that it is possible for true Christians to allow themselves to get into such a terribly cold and backslidden condition that, for a while, they do not live as they should.

While backsliding is indeed prevalent, I think the second answer is more often the explanation—that many of these people are simply not Christians at all! They think they are, but they are not! They believe they have been delivered from hell, but every day off the calendar moves them one step closer to it. Becoming a Christian is not a matter of walking an aisle, being baptized, and getting one's name in a church book. It is a matter of having so encountered the living God that one's life is changed. If there is no change, there is no Christianity! It is as simple and as frightening as that!

The sad truth is many expect their so-called Christianity to get them to heaven, and yet it won't even get them to church! These poor people will not realize their true state until that day they expect to enter heaven only to hear the Lord Jesus say: "I never knew you; depart from Me…" (Matt. 7:23).

All of Christianity can be boiled down to three words: GUILT, GRACE and GRATITUDE. All of us have the guilt—the guilt of sin. But only Christians have the grace and the gratitude. All Christians have received God's grace in salvation, and all express their gratitude. If there is no gratitude, it is because there is no grace!

-18-

From God's Word, the Bible...

"Because I live, you will live also. At that day you will know that I am in My Father, and you in Me, and I in you."
Now Jesus knew that they desired to ask Him, and He said to them, "Are you inquiring among yourselves about what I said, 'A little while, and you will not see Me; and again a little while, and you will see Me'? Most assuredly, I say to you that you will weep and lament, but the world will rejoice; and you will be sorrowful, but your sorrow will be turned into joy. A woman, when she is in labor, has sorrow because her hour has come; but as soon as she has given birth to the child, she no longer remembers the anguish, for joy that a human being has been born into the world. Therefore you now have sorrow; but I will see you again and your heart will rejoice, and your joy no one will take from you."

From John 14:19,20; John 16:16-22

What to Preach on at Easter

Several years ago, a distraught woman asked if she could talk with me about a matter that was weighing heavily on her mind and heart. A member of a mega-church, she was troubled by what she heard her pastor say on Easter Sunday. With thousands present, he began his message with these words:

"I realize it is Easter, and you all are expecting to hear a sermon about the resurrection, but I want to preach on something more relevant." He then proceeded to deliver a message about modern-day family living!

I assured her that she was right to be troubled. If we were all destined to continue to live on this earth the same kind of lives that we are living now, a message on some aspect of life in this world would be very relevant indeed. But, there's the rub! Our lives on this earth do not stretch out endlessly!

They have an end to them. We all have an appointment with death (Heb. 9:27).

I certainly have nothing against a preacher talking about the importance of the family or some other aspect of living in this world. Such subjects must be addressed because the Bible itself addresses them. The problem is that many preachers these days are talking *exclusively* about such topics. To hear them preach, one would never get the impression that death is racing toward us and eternity is opening its arms to receive us.

Because death is always the greatest fact of life, I am not in a dilemma about what I will preach on Easter. The resurrection of Jesus will be my theme!

What relevance does the resurrection of Jesus have for dying people? Much! By His resurrection, Jesus proved Himself to be exactly what He claimed to be—God in human flesh (Rom. 1:4). If He is God, He cannot lie (Num. 23:19; Titus 1:2). If He cannot lie, the words He spoke to Martha must come true: "I am the resurrection and the life. He who believes in Me, though he may die, he shall live" (John 11:25).

Because Jesus arose from the grave, those who believe in Him as their Lord and Savior do not have to worry about death. It will not have the final word regarding them. The Lord Jesus will raise their bodies from their graves (1 Thess. 4:14-16) and give them bodies fashioned after His own resurrection body (Phil. 3:20-21).

His victory over death guarantees their victory over death. He Himself says to all His people: "Because I live, you will live also" (John 14:19). The Apostle Paul assured the Christians in Rome of this truth by writing: "He who raised Christ from the dead will also give life to your mortal bodies through the Spirit who dwells in you" (Rom. 8:11).

Thomas Watson, one of the Puritans, triumphantly affirmed the resurrection of God's people in these memorable words: "We are more sure to rise out of our grave than out of our beds."

Something more relevant than the resurrection of Jesus? I think not! As a dying man, I will again next Easter look to the resurrection of Jesus as my hope and my joy. If the resurrection of Jesus is irrelevant, let me be irrelevant this Easter and every other day!

-19-

From God's Word, the Bible...

And you know that He was manifested to take away our sins, and in Him there is no sin.

1 John 3:5

What about Hypocrites in the Church?

Our English word "hypocrite" comes from the Greek word "hupocrites." That word was used for Greek and Roman actors who covered their faces and distorted their voices so that they appeared to be someone other than themselves.

These actors had two faces. One was the face behind the mask, and the other was the face of the mask. The two were, of course, quite different.

From that simple beginning the word came to be applied to anyone who pretends to be something he is not. The person himself is one way, but he holds up a mask, as it were, to hide the reality and to give the impression that he is someone quite different.

Jesus charged the Pharisees with hypocrisy. They wanted to give the impression that they loved God, but Jesus knew there was no real love for God in them but only love for themselves.

No charge is more frequently leveled against Christians today than that of hypocrisy, and many unbelievers use the hypocrisy of believers, whether perceived or real, as their reason for rejecting Christ.

This is, then, an issue that we cannot ignore. How should Christians respond to the issue of hypocrisy?

We must first point out the simple truth that not all are Christians who claim to be. The fact that one *professes* faith in Christ does not mean that he actually *possesses* faith in Christ.

We should always remember that the Bible gives several warnings about the matter of being deceived (Matt. 7:21-23; 2 Cor. 13:5; 2 Peter 1:10) as well as examples of men who were deceived about their faith (Judas, Demas). The Bible also gives us certain tests we can use to determine if we are truly saved (1 John). All of this would be pointless unless it is terribly possible to think we are saved when we are not.

In the second place, we must point out that the Bible's teaching about Christians is far different than the popular understanding of Christians. In other words, people who accuse Christians of hypocrisy often employ a higher standard for Christian behavior than does the Bible.

The Bible teaches that conversion makes a profound and lasting change in the individual, but it does not teach that the Christian will ever attain perfection in this life. To the contrary, the Bible teaches the reality of indwelling sin in the life of the Christian and the ongoing conflict the Christian has with sin.

The Christian will never be completely free from sin in this life. He is a work in progress. He has been forgiven of his sins and made right with God (an act of God called *justification*). He is now growing and maturing (a process called *sanctification*). He will finally be freed from sin and made like Christ (an event called *glorification*).

Someone put it like this: "I am not what I ought to be. I am not what I am going to be. But, thank God, I am not what I used to be."

When unbelievers see evidence of imperfection in the Christian, they are seeing the truth of the Bible confirmed!

By the way, Jesus Himself clearly indicated that hypocrites would be found wherever true faith is found (Matt. 24:11,24), and, as noted above, even had a hypocrite among His disciples.

In the third place, we should point out that all hypocrites will finally be exposed and judged.

Every Christian is hypocritical to some extent because no Christian is perfect. But those who, on the one hand, continually show themselves to be hypocrites and, on the other hand, are never troubled by their failures, never repent, and never give any evidence of genuine faith will experience the fulfillment of the Lord's promise of judgment (Luke 12:1-5).

Finally, we must always be eager to say that the Lord Jesus Christ was not a hypocrite.

The question each unbeliever must face is not whether Christians are hypocrites, but whether Jesus was a hypocrite. We are not saved by other Christians; we are saved by Jesus!

Those who closely study the life of Jesus find no evidence of failure or sin in Him but rather find themselves taking as their own the words of Pontius Pilate, who said of Jesus: "I find no fault in Him" (John 19:6).

-20-

From God's Word, the Bible...

Trust in the LORD with all your heart,
And lean not on your own understanding;
In all your ways acknowledge Him,
And He shall direct your paths.

Proverbs 3:5,6

Finding God's Will

Christians know several things about this matter of finding and understanding the will of God:

- God has a will for their lives—that is, He does care how they live.
- He does not merely shrug and say: "Do what you want." God's will is right and good. Christians fully subscribe to Paul's teaching that the will of God is "good and acceptable and perfect" (Rom. 12:2).
- They must eventually stand before God and give account of the way in which they lived (Rom. 14:12). Those who live most completely in line with the will of God will be much more at peace on that day.

The main problems Christians face on the matter of the will of God are discovering it and carrying it out. This devotional reading is designed to help with the first of these problems.

How can we know the will of God for our lives? The first thing for us to do probably sounds strange. We must relax! We have a tendency to think that discovering the will of God depends entirely on us, but the truth is that the Lord leads His children far more than they realize (Ps. 23:1-3; 32:8; 37:23; Rom. 8:14; Phil. 2:13).

The second thing for us to do is read and study the Bible.

- The Bible lays out God's purpose for each of His children, namely, living in such a way as to bring honor to Him (1 Peter 2:9-10).
- The Bible gives us direct commandments and prohibitions (e.g., The Ten Commandments).
- The Bible gives us a pattern to follow (Phil. 2:5-11).
- The Bible and the Holy Spirit always agree.

The third thing for us to do is refocus. If we primarily focus our attention on being the right kind of people and on performing the duties that God has assigned to us, the will of God will find us.

Proverbs 3:5-6 teaches us to occupy ourselves with trusting in the Lord and acknowledging Him in all our ways. If we will do these things, we can be assured that the Lord will direct our paths.

Adrian Rogers captured this truth in these words: "The will of God is not a *road map*; it is a *relationship*…"

What is the outcome of acknowledging God in all our ways? Charles Bridges says: "No step well prayed over will bring ultimate regret. Though the promise will not rend us infallible; our very error will be overruled for deeper humiliation and self-knowledge; and thus even this mysterious direction will in the end be gratefully acknowledged, 'He led me forth in the right way'." (Ps. 107:7).

The final thing for us to do is ask. The Bible assures us

that God will grant us wisdom if we will ask Him for it (James 1:5).

In praying about the will of God, we should also hold before God His promises to guide His people, as the hymnwriter did in these lines:

> *I need Thee every hour, most gracious Lord;*
> *No tender voice like Thine can peace afford.*
> *I need Thee every hour, teach me Thy will;*
> *Thy promise so rich in me fulfill.*

Here are some other guidelines that will help us on this matter of finding God's will:

- If we want to know more of the will of God, we must practice those things which we already know to be His will. God is not obligated to reveal more of His will to those who are disregarding that which He has already revealed.
- We must be careful about assuming how God will lead—that is, we must not think that God's will is always the most unpleasant course of action. God gives us certain desires and inclinations and then works through those desires. On the other hand, we must not assume that the will of God is easy and problem free.
- Consult circumstances, spiritual leaders, and spiritual friends.
- Be patient. We tend to be great believers in instant gratification, but God does not work according to our schedules.

-21-

From God's Word, the Bible...

"If you had known Me, you would have known My Father also; and from now on you know Him and have seen Him."
Philip said to Him, "Lord, show us the Father, and it is sufficient for us."
Jesus said to him, "Have I been with you so long, and yet you have not known Me, Philip? He who has seen Me has seen the Father; so how can you say, 'Show us the Father'? Do you not believe that I am in the Father, and the Father in Me? The words that I speak to you I do not speak on My own authority; but the Father who dwells in Me does the works. Believe Me that I am in the Father and the Father in Me, or else believe Me for the sake of the works themselves.

John 14:7-11

How Can We Be Sure God Exists?

There is no need to belabor the importance of this question. Everyone is agreed on its importance. If God exists, this world is one kind of world; if He does not, it is a radically different kind. If God exists, we are one kind of being; if He does not, we are a far different kind. If God exists, we are required to live one kind of life; if He does not, we can live an entirely different kind. If God exists, we have one kind of future; if He does not, we have a totally different kind.

The question, then, is not the importance of the question! It is rather how we can know for sure that God exists.

It is interesting that the Bible does not argue for the existence of God but assumes it (Gen. 1:1). It does not debate with the atheist, but rather dismisses such a person (Ps. 14:1).

This dismissal is not due to a lack of evidence for God

but rather to such an abundance of evidence that the atheist does not have a leg on which to stand. God has not left Himself without witness! (See Acts 14:17.)

The created order itself gives powerful testimony to God (Ps. 19:1-6; Acts 14:15-16; Rom. 1:18-20).

Don Fortner has rightly observed: "Three things are revealed to all men in creation which cannot be denied. The Book of God declares that all men know these three things about God; (1) God is (2) God is wise (3) God is almighty."

The witness of the created order to God compelled Abraham Lincoln to say: "I cannot conceive of how any man could look up into the heavens and say there is no God."

God has also left witness to Himself by giving each individual an intuitive knowledge that He, God, exists, that we are His creatures and must eventually give account of ourselves to Him. The Apostle Paul tells us that this knowledge is so powerful that the only way it can be silenced is for men to "suppress" it (Rom. 1:18-19). The word "suppress" suggests putting the truth in a box and nailing the lid shut!

The outer testimony of creation and the inner testimony of conscience are compelling and persuasive, but the most definitive proof of God is Christ.

The Lord Jesus Christ claimed to be God in human flesh (John 14:7-11). He claimed to be sent by God (John 7:28-29; 8:42), to exercise the prerogatives of God (John 5:21-23,25-27), to do the works of God (John 10:37-38) and to speak for God (John 12:49-50).

The Apostle John, who was closely associated with Jesus for more than three years, also affirmed that He was God (John 1:14,18; 1 John 1:1-2).

The miracles of Jesus prove that He was God. These miracles were great in number, were of all types, and were witnessed by multitudes.

The teachings of Jesus indicated that He was God (Matt.

7:28-29; 13:54; John 7:46).

The many prophecies He fulfilled give us yet another proof of Jesus' deity, and His resurrection from the dead is the towering, crowning proof that He was God (Rom. 1:4).

Here is the point: if Jesus was God, God exists!

All the proofs for the existence of God, powerful and persuasive as they are, will not convince people of the existence of God. They may help us to win the argument, but they will not help us to win the sinner (1 Cor. 2:14). That work can only be accomplished by the Holy Spirit of God. The Apostle Paul declares: "…no one can say that Jesus is Lord except by the Holy Spirit" (1 Cor. 12:3).

We must recognize that people do not disbelieve in God because they have intellectual problems that they cannot resolve, but because they have a spiritual problem they won't face. They don't believe in God because they don't want there to be a God. Only the Spirit of God can change their hearts.

We Christians have another problem. Because the Spirit of God has worked in our hearts, we do not need to be convinced of the existence of God. Our need is to feel passion for the God whose existence we acknowledge—to feel such passion that we will live for His glory.

-22-

From God's Word, the Bible...

And they all cried out at once, saying, "Away with this Man, and release to us Barabbas"—who had been thrown into prison for a certain rebellion made in the city, and for murder.
Pilate, therefore, wishing to release Jesus, again called out to them. But they shouted, saying, "Crucify Him, crucify Him!"
Then he said to them the third time, "Why, what evil has He done? I have found no reason for death in Him. I will therefore chastise Him and let Him go." But they were insistent, demanding with loud voices that He be crucified. And the voices of these men and of the chief priests prevailed. So Pilate gave sentence that it should be as they requested. And he released to them the one they requested, who for rebellion and murder had been thrown into prison; but he delivered Jesus to their will.

From Luke 23:13-25

Just Call Me Barabbas

Barabbas was a dead man, and Pilate was a desperate man. I say Barabbas was a dead man because he had been condemned to die. He was found guilty of insurrection and murder. The sentence had been handed down and only a few dreary hours were lying between Barabbas and the execution of that sentence.

Pilate, on the other hand, was a desperate man. The Jewish leaders were demanding that Jesus be crucified, and Pilate knew that Jesus had done nothing to deserve such a fate. So Pilate was in a dilemma and desperate to get out of it.

But Pilate was also a clever man. He would give the Jews a choice! He would bring both Jesus and Barabbas before the people and let them decide who would be released and who would be crucified.

As far as Pilate was concerned, it was a no-brainer. The

people would choose Jesus, the man who had gone about healing the sick, casting out demons, and proclaiming the kingdom of God. Barabbas, on the other hand, was such a low-life character that all would be glad to be rid of him.

It was perfect! Barabbas the guilty would receive the death he deserved, and Jesus the innocent would go free.

After many hours of tossing and turning, Barabbas finally falls asleep. But suddenly he is awakened by the clanking of armor and the loud talking of Roman soldiers. They are on their way to get him, and he is on his way to the cross!

But much to his surprise, Barabbas finds himself being escorted to Pilate's hall. What is going on? Barabbas soon has his answer. He is standing on a balcony with Pilate and a man named Jesus, and Pilate is asking the large throng below to choose whether he, Barabbas, or Jesus should be released!

There is no doubt in Barabbas' mind on how this is going to turn out! The multitude will choose Jesus, and he will keep his appointment with the cross. The only thing this would change is the time. He will be crucified a bit later but still crucified.

Now to his amazement he hears the crowd crying, "We want Barabbas!" And Pilate, equally astonished, asks: "What shall I do with Jesus?" And the crowd angrily shouts: "Crucify Him! Crucify Him!"

Pilate turns to a soldier and says: "Release Barabbas and prepare Jesus for crucifixion."

Barabbas is not quite sure what to do with himself. He finally decides to follow the crowd out to Golgotha. And now they are hoisting the cross on which Jesus had been nailed, and Barabbas says to himself: "I would have been there had Jesus not been put in my place."

My name is Barabbas. As he was guilty of breaking the laws of the Roman government, I stand guilty of breaking

God's laws. As he was justly condemned to physical death, I have been justly condemned to eternal death. But as Barabbas' place on the cross was taken by Jesus, so my place was taken by Jesus. Yes, my name is Barabbas. Jesus died in my place, receiving the eternal wrath I deserve. And now there is no penalty left for me to pay. Oh, my heart, rejoice!

-23-

From God's Word, the Bible...

"I do not receive honor from men. But I know you, that you do not have the love of God in you. I have come in My Father's name, and you do not receive Me; if another comes in his own name, him you will receive. How can you believe, who receive honor from one another, and do not seek the honor that comes from the only God? Do not think that I shall accuse you to the Father; there is one who accuses you—Moses, in whom you trust. For if you believed Moses, you would believe Me; for he wrote about Me. But if you do not believe his writings, how will you believe My words?"

From John 5:31-47

A Crisis of Faith

Several years ago I experienced a crisis of faith that was so severe that I was not sure whether I could continue to embrace Christianity. I look back at that time now with embarrassment. I thought at the time that my faith was something that I was holding, and I wasn't sure whether I could keep my grip. Now I realize that it was my faith that was holding me.

The one issue that held me was the Gospel accounts of the life and ministry of Jesus. I could not get around the evidence for Him. I found Him inescapably to be the Christ. The only conclusion that made sense to me was that He was God in human flesh. His miraculous deeds and His powerful and astounding teachings, all of which were substantiated by numerous witnesses, left me no room to maneuver. I had tried to get away from Him, but He pursued and conquered me.

I still do not have all the answers that I would like. I am not a Christian because Christianity answers all my questions. I am a Christian because Christianity gives me answers that I cannot get around. Somewhere along life's journey, it occurred to me that the truth about Jesus is so strong and compelling that I could safely put my questions in my hip pocket until I enter heaven's glory. There in His presence, I expect to finally get them answered, and I expect to find that the answers will all make perfect sense. I also expect to feel no little embarrassment over allowing such things to trouble me.

I recall that Nathanael originally thought he could not accept Jesus as the Messiah because Jesus was from Nazareth, but at Philip's insistence, he, Nathanael, agreed to see Jesus. When Jesus told him that He had seen him under the fig tree before Philip ever spoke to him, Nathanael realized the truth. Jesus was indeed the Messiah (John 1:43-51). It's interesting to me that Nathanael accepted Jesus as the Messiah without ever getting his Nazareth problem resolved. The evidence for Jesus overwhelmed Nathanael. He realized that he could wait to get his Nazareth question answered. He could not wait to confess the truth about Jesus.

Like Nathanael, I have my Nazareth issues, but the evidence for Jesus overwhelms them—and me! The miracles He performed, the words that He spoke, the lives that He changed, the prophecies He fulfilled, and His resurrection all tell me that He was God in human flesh and that He is worthy of my love and devotion. It is not merely that I choose to believe in Jesus. It is rather that I must believe in Him.

I trust that, by the grace of God, I have learned to believe my beliefs and doubt my doubts. I believe in Jesus. I believe that He, the second Person of the Trinity, came to this earth in our humanity. I believe that He died a special kind of death, one such as no one before or since has died. I believe that on the cross He received the wrath of God in my stead so that I will never have to experience that wrath myself. I believe that He arose from the dead and lives today to make intercession for His people. I believe that He gave the Holy Spirit to His people to guide, comfort, strengthen and encourage them. I believe that I will see Him when He comes again and will marvel at the sight of His nail-pierced hands and wounded side. I believe that I will be made like Him and in the ceaseless ages of eternity will be lost in wonder, love and praise.

Yes, I believe in Jesus.

-24-

From God's Word, the Bible...

"Do not lay up for yourselves treasures on earth, where moth and rust destroy and where thieves break in and steal; but lay up for yourselves treasures in heaven, where neither moth nor rust destroys and where thieves do not break in and steal. For where your treasure is, there your heart will be also.

Matthew 6:19-21

Weird Things

Do you pay attention to some of the weird things that take place and are reported in the news? I heard a couple of very weird things reported some time ago. One is the story of a man who was so elated that the New York Jets defeated the New England Patriots that he jumped on his sled and went speeding down his icy driveway right out into the street where he was hit by a car and killed! He was so happy over one game that he didn't get to see the next game!

Another news report showed a clip of a young woman who was so engrossed in texting as she walked along that she fell into a pool!

It is not hard to see what these stories have in common. These people were so caught up in the moment that they did not see any danger. Isolated incidents? Not at all! Our nation is filled with people who are very much like the two in these stories. They are so caught up in the here and now that they don't think about the reality and the danger of the Judgment

Day that is lying ahead, and they are making no preparation for it.

Another story that comes to my mind is that of the death of Don Meredith, who was fond of wrapping up the games on Monday Night Football with the words, "Turn out the lights, the party's over." Those who are so engaged with the here and now would do well to reflect on those words. Life in this world is coming to an end. The lights will soon be turned out, the party will be over, and it will be time to meet God! How we need to heed these words from Jesus: "Do not labor for the food which perishes, but for the food which endures to everlasting life..." (John 6:27).

Then there is the story of Arthur Stace. Born to alcoholic parents and in deep poverty, Arthur was converted on the night of August 6, 1930, at St. Barnabas Church in Sydney, Australia.

Two years later he heard Reverend John Ridley say: "Eternity, Eternity, I wish that I could sound or shout that word to everyone in the streets of Sydney. You've got to meet it; where will you spend Eternity?"

Arthur would later say: "Eternity went ringing through my brain and suddenly I began crying and felt a powerful call from the Lord to write Eternity."

So write it he did. So night after night he would walk around his city and write the word ETERNITY in chalk wherever he could find a spot. Arthur did not do this for just a week, a month or a year. He stayed with it year after year. It was finally estimated that he wrote that single word in public places at least 500,000 times in thirty-five years.

For a long time, the citizens of Sydney did not know the name of the person who was filling their city with this single word. As they saw it time after time, they must have wondered who was writing it. Finally, a reporter solved the mystery. It was Arthur Stace. From then on, Arthur was called Mr. Eternity.

We can be sure of two things. One is that Arthur Stace lived with the daily awareness of eternity. The other is that he caused many others to be aware of it as well.

Arthur died on July 30, 1967, finally entering into the eternal glory that was so much on his mind in this life.

Some would call him weird, but the truly weird thing is not to live thinking about eternity but rather to live without thinking about it and preparing for it. And the only way to prepare for it is by trusting in the Lord Jesus Christ.

-25-

From God's Word, the Bible...

Who among you will give ear to this?
Who will listen and hear for the time to come?
Who gave Jacob for plunder, and Israel to the robbers?
Was it not the LORD,
He against whom we have sinned?
For they would not walk in His ways,
Nor were they obedient to His law.
Therefore He has poured on him the fury of His anger
And the strength of battle;
It has set him on fire all around,
Yet he did not know;
And it burned him,
Yet he did not take it to heart.

Isaiah 42:23-25

When It Happens

I include myself in the category of the many who think our nation may very well be headed toward unprecedented calamity. I do not know whether that calamity will consist of a terrorist attack, a natural disaster, an epidemic, a complete financial collapse or some combination of these things.

I do know this—if and when such a calamity occurs, many will cry out: "How could God let this happen?"

That, I suggest, will be the wrong question. The right question will be: "How could we let this happen?"

God has placed us in this world and has given us a very definite and distinct assignment. We are to live for His glory. We do this by obeying His commandments. When we live as God commands, we bring blessings into our lives. When we refuse to do so, we invite Him to judge us. In other words, we invite Him to send calamity upon us.

How are we doing with this matter of living in this world as God has commanded? Not well! Consider the following:

- We consistently treat God's name as if it were a light and trivial thing instead of something to be reverenced.
- We consistently use God's day as if it were designed for us to do those things that bring us pleasure. How frequently God's house is forsaken these days for the flimsiest reasons!
- Many who do attend church choose services for their entertainment value and emotional appeal instead of their commitment to faithfully expounding the Word of God and declaring the gospel of Jesus Christ.
- Multitudes who attend church do so without any real warmth in their hearts toward the truths of God. In so doing, they make themselves like the Pharisees who drew near to God with their lips while their hearts were far from Him.

The list could go on and on.

God is so patient and kind that He does not send calamity upon us as soon as we begin breaking His laws. He gives us ample opportunities to repent and turn back to Him. But there is a limit to His patience, and when the end comes, His judgment will most certainly fall. When it does, the blame should not be placed on the God who told us how to live and who patiently put up with our sins. It should rather be placed on us for stubbornly refusing to live as God commanded and for spurning His repeated calls to us to repent.

What is repentance? Although it does not use the word, Psalm 119:59 gives us a wonderful definition:

> *I thought about my ways*
> *And turned my feet to Your testimonies.*

The psalmist speaks of turning his feet toward God's testimonies. We all know that it is impossible to turn toward something without simultaneously turning away from something. To turn toward God, then, is to turn away from the thing that is opposed to God. What is that thing? It is sin. To repent is to turn away from sin and to turn toward God. It is to do an about face.

We can picture it in this way. Before we repent, our faces are toward our sin and our backs toward God. In repenting, we turn our backs toward our sins and our faces toward God.

Repentance is to think so deeply and seriously about our sins that we change our behavior. And there is absolutely no point in claiming that we have repented if we have not turned our backs on our sins. The amazing thing is that when we turn our backs on our sins, God puts our sins behind His back (Isa. 38:17). The Bible also tells us that true repentance means:

- God buries our sins in the depths of the sea (Micah 7:19)
- God sweeps away our sins (Isa. 44:22)
- God removes our sins as far as the east is from the west (Ps. 103:12)
- God forgives our sins and remembers them no more (Jer. 31:34)

The hope for our nation lies in recovering true Christianity, and the hope for recovering true Christianity lies largely in Christians repenting of their sins and beginning to live again as they should have been living all along.

-26-

From God's Word, the Bible...

Live joyfully with the wife whom you love all the days of your vain life which He has given you under the sun, all your days of vanity; for that is your portion in life, and in the labor which you perform under the sun. Whatever your hand finds to do, do it with your might; for there is no work or device or knowledge or wisdom in the grave where you are going. Rejoice, O young man, in your youth, And let your heart cheer you in the days of your youth; Walk in the ways of your heart, And in the sight of your eyes; But know that for all these God will bring you into judgment. Therefore remove sorrow from your heart, And put away evil from your flesh, For childhood and youth are vanity.

Ecclesiastes 9:9-10; 11:9-10

Savoring

Adam and Eve were the first to eat of the tree of knowledge of good and evil. All of us have been eating of it ever since.

Life in this world is a mixture of good and evil. Much of our time is consumed with the evil side. We constantly hear about it: terrorism, war, conflict, political corruption, family fragmentation, hunger, child abuse, abortion, and pornography. The list goes on and on. The news reports are essentially the evil reports.

We all have to wage our personal battles with evil. We are constantly prone to lie, cheat, lust, steal, and hate. We also have a firm antipathy to doing the things that God commands us to do. We often find ourselves clenched in a vise with two jaws: the one is commission of the wrong; the other is omission of the good.

But that is only part of the story. We know evil in other ways. We get sick. Family members get sick and die. We struggle to get along with others. And finally we die. Life is a journey, and death is its end.

Because we eat so much evil from life's tree, it is entirely possible for us to become so absorbed with it that we fail to appreciate the good. As fallen creatures, we do not savor the good of life to the degree that we should.

I have often remarked that the thing that has surprised me most about life is how fast it goes. It passes with blinding speed. It is very easy to come to its end with searing regret. We may very well regret the evil we have done and the good we have failed to do. A good part of our regret may be the good we failed to savor.

For a lot of people, life is something that happens while they are busy with other things. I don't want life just to happen. I want to savor it, and I want to help others savor it as well.

By the way, to savor something is to give ourselves to the enjoyment of it. How many of life's truly significant moments pass without our realizing their significance! When Sylvia and I had little boys, a part of each day was spent picking them up and carrying them. There were times when it was inconvenient. But our little boys grew, and one day, without realizing it, I put each one down, never to pick him up again. I have often thought that if I had known that I was holding my sons in my arms for the last time, I would have held them a lot longer. I would have savored the moment.

In calling you to savor the good things of this world, I am not suggesting that you live as if this world is all that there is. Quite the opposite! Nothing so enhances our enjoyment of this world as the confidence that we are prepared for the next. By the way, that world, free as it will be from all sin and sorrow, will be the place where we will truly and fully savor our new life. And the only way to enter that world is through faith in Christ. Here is a touch of irony for you—it is only as we look beyond this world to that better world that we are truly able to enjoy our *present* world.

So I call you to savor the good things of this world as well as those things that prepare us for the next—savor God, the glorious gospel of Christ, the Bible, the preaching of the Bible, the church, the beauties of creation, the privilege of worship, marriage, and children. Let us always seek to remember these words from Stephen Vincent Benet: "Life is not lost by dying. It is lost moment by moment in a thousand uncaring ways."

Then there are these words from Thomas S. Monson: "The past is behind; learn from it. The future is ahead; prepare for it. The present is here; live it."

-27-

From God's Word, the Bible...

For I know the thoughts that I think toward you, says the LORD, thoughts of peace and not of evil, to give you a future and a hope.

Jeremiah 29:11

"Trusting in My Father's Wise Bestowment..."

Day by day, and with each passing moment,
Strength I find to meet my trials here;
Trusting in my Father's wise bestowment,
I've no cause for worry or for fear.
He, whose heart is kind beyond all measure,
Gives unto each day what He deems best,
Lovingly its part of pain and pleasure,
Mingling toil with peace and rest.

(*Day by Day*, Lina Sandell)

Lina Sandell knew about trials, having seen her father, a Lutheran pastor, fall from the boat in which they were sailing and drown. We might be inclined to think that such a heartbreaking event would have caused this young woman (she was twenty-six at the time) to renounce her faith in God. Harsh questions must have besieged her. Could God not have prevented this tragedy? If so, why would He allow it to happen? And why would He allow it to happen to a family who loved and served Him?

Amazingly, Lina Sandell found comfort in God. Specifically, she found comfort in His "wise bestowment." How much is packed in those two words! With the word "bestowment," Lina was registering her conviction that the Christian's trials do not come because of lapses or breakdowns in God's governance of the universe. There are no cracks in heaven for things to slip through! Our trials come to us because our Father in heaven bestows them upon us. He gives them to us.

Why would God make such bestowments? That's where the word "wise" must come in. God governs our circumstances with infinite wisdom. We are not going to understand God's working in our lives if we insist on believing that God's major concern is to bring us as much comfort and ease as possible. But what if God's concern is to conform us to the image of His Son (Rom. 8:29)? What if God is seeking our spiritual maturity instead of our temporal happiness? Does it not make sense to say that God will govern our lives one way if He is seeking our ease and a totally different way if He is seeking our maturity?

Lina Sandell was undoubtedly familiar with the Old Testament account of Joseph. What bestowments Joseph experienced! Hated by his brothers! Sold into slavery! Falsely accused and wrongly imprisoned! But through these wise bestowments, God was wisely at work to further His plan.

(You can read about this in Genesis 50:20.)

"But I don't see how this circumstance could possibly further God's plan," is the common response of many people when it comes to their trials. That's where the trusting must take place. The Bible doesn't tell us that we will always understand what God is doing in a particular situation. It does tell us that God is working all things together for our good (Rom. 8:28).

Is God's heart really "kind beyond all measure"? How can we tell? Most of us tend to look at our circumstances. If they are good, we conclude that God is kind. If they are not good, we can find ourselves wondering if He is.

There is only one place to look to determine how God feels about His people, and that is the cross of Christ. God the Father put His Son on that cross—and the Son gladly and willingly went there—to rescue His people from eternal death and to give them eternal life.

That is the greatest thing God could ever do for us, and He has done it. That decisively proves His kindness. If He has done this great thing for us, are we going to allow ourselves when our circumstances turn sour to conclude that God has withdrawn His kindness? If God in kindness paid such a dear price for our salvation, are we going to entertain for a moment the notion that He is no longer kind? Why would He make the supreme expression of kindness to deal with our biggest problem—sin—only to withhold kindness in all the lesser problems that come our way? The Apostle Paul uses this logic in Romans 8:32: "He who did not spare His own Son, but delivered Him up for us all, how shall He not with Him also freely give us all things?"

All Christians want to have a strong faith. We know our faith is getting strong when we are able to believe that those very circumstances that seem to indicate that God is not kind are, in fact, proofs that He is.

-28-

From God's Word, the Bible...

Moreover, brethren, I declare to you the gospel which I preached to you, which also you received and in which you stand, by which also you are saved, if you hold fast that word which I preached to you—unless you believed in vain. For I delivered to you first of all that which I also received: that Christ died for our sins according to the Scriptures, and that He was buried, and that He rose again the third day according to the Scriptures, and that He was seen by Cephas, then by the twelve. After that He was seen by over five hundred brethren at once, of whom the greater part remain to the present, but some have fallen asleep. After that He was seen by James, then by all the apostles. Then last of all He was seen by me also, as by one born out of due time.

1 Corinthians 15:1-8

Turtles All the Way Down

A teacher asked her class why the earth doesn't fall. One boy answered: "Because it is sitting on the back of a turtle."

"And what keeps that turtle from falling?" asked the teacher.

The boy said: "Because it is sitting on the back of another turtle."

That, of course, led the teacher to ask: "And what keeps that turtle from falling?"

Deciding to put the back-and-forth conversation to an end, the boy responded: "It's turtles all the way down."

How this boy determined that the earth sits atop a huge stack of turtles is unknown!

Christians believe in the resurrection of Jesus. It is the centerpiece of their faith. Multitudes in these skeptical days put the belief of Christians in the resurrection in the same category as the boy and his turtles. As far as they are concerned, the two are one and the same. The resurrection and the turtles belong in the fantasy category! The boy invented his turtles, and Christians have invented the resurrection!

Skeptics are ever eager to put the resurrection into the turtle category because they know where it would lead if it were in the "it really happened" category—that would lead them where they do not want to go! It would cause them to admit that Jesus was God in human flesh, that what He says is true, and that He is worthy of our worship and devotion. So they deny, deny, deny.

The Apostle Paul had the resurrection of Jesus firmly in the turtle category for a considerable time. Regarding Christians as both deluded and dangerous, he decided to make it his life's work to rid his world of them. But on his way to Damascus he was hit with evidence that he could not ignore. The resurrected, living Christ appeared to him and moved his thinking from the turtle category to the reality category (Acts 9).

The little boy evidently believed in the stack of turtles because that is what he wanted to believe. He had no evidence for it, but Christians do not believe in the resurrection of Jesus merely because they want to. No, the risen Christ has not appeared to each and every Christian as He did to Paul, but there is still plenty of evidence. The heavy stone sealing the tomb was rolled away, angels were present, the Roman guards were in something of a stupor, the tomb was empty, and the linen strips in which the body of Jesus was wrapped were in a convincing configuration (Matt. 28, Mark 16, Luke 24, John 20). And the risen Christ began appearing to His disciples. He even appeared to five hundred people on one occasion (1 Cor. 15:6).

All of these evidences led the Lord Chief Justice of England, Lord Darlington, to observe: "No intelligent jury in the world could fail to bring in a verdict that the resurrection story is true."

Dr. Paul L. Maier, professor of ancient history at Western Michigan University, adds: "If all the evidence is weighed carefully and fairly, it is indeed justifiable according to the canons of historical research, to conclude that the tomb in which Jesus was buried was actually empty on the morning of the first Easter…. No shred of evidence has been discovered which would disprove this statement."

Christians merely ask skeptics to admit that there is convincing evidence for Jesus' resurrection and not to put us in the turtle category for going where that evidence leads. We further ask skeptics to admit that their refusal to believe in the resurrection does not have to do with lack of evidence but with an unwillingness to go where that evidence leads. Harvard law professor, Simon Greenleaf, says: "All that Christianity asks of men … is, that they would be consistent with themselves; that they would treat its evidences as they treat the evidence of other things…"

Do you believe in the truth of the resurrection of Jesus? You may have full confidence in the Bible's account!

-29-

From God's Word, the Bible...

But He said to him, "Man, who made Me a judge or an arbitrator over you?" And He said to them, "Take heed and beware of covetousness, for one's life does not consist in the abundance of the things he possesses." Then He spoke a parable to them, saying: "The ground of a certain rich man yielded plentifully. And he thought within himself, saying, 'What shall I do, since I have no room to store my crops?' So he said, 'I will do this: I will pull down my barns and build greater, and there I will store all my crops and my goods. And I will say to my soul, "Soul, you have many goods laid up for many years; take your ease; eat, drink, and be merry."' But God said to him, 'Fool! This night your soul will be required of you; then whose will those things be which you have provided?' So is he who lays up treasure for himself, and is not rich toward God."

Luke 12:14-21

True Riches

Jesus tells a story about a farmer who raises such a bumper crop that he has no place to store it. He decides to solve the problem by replacing his old barns with greater ones.

There is nothing wrong with this man taking thought to the matter of storing his crop or with him planning to build larger barns. The wrong comes in what he goes on to say: "And I will say to my soul, 'Soul, you have many goods laid up for many years; take your ease; eat, drink, and be merry.'"

Here is a statement of glaring omissions. No thought is given to the uncertain nature of earthly riches. We can have them one day, and they can be gone the next! This man acts as if he can count on them.

No thought is given to the certainty of death. He acts as if he will be on this earth forever. He does not hear the steady footfall of approaching death.

Nothing is said to indicate that he regards his wealth as a stewardship with which to honor God and bring blessing to others. No thought is given to God as the Giver of the bounty he enjoys and as the One before whom he must finally stand and give account.

It is obvious that this man is counting on his crop, his barns, and a long string of days with which to enjoy them. The thing he is not counting on is what happens. He hears the voice of God: "You fool! This night your soul will be required of you; then whose will those things be which you have provided?"

Now his crops and his barns are all worthless. They have no power to help him. They cannot stave off death, and they cannot prepare him for the eternity into which he must go. Now he wishes he had thought less about preparing for his ease and more about preparing his soul.

Jesus' story, then, is about the folly of allowing ourselves to be so consumed with the things of this world that we fail to be rich toward God.

What does it mean to be rich toward God? It means to be rich in knowledge, knowing God is our Creator and will finally be our Judge, and knowing that He is a holy God and demands that we be holy as well. It is being rich in the knowledge of ourselves, realizing that we do not possess the righteousness God demands but are, in fact, sinners. It is being rich in the knowledge of the grace of God, knowing that He, the holy God, is also the God of infinite grace. It is being rich in the knowledge of Christ, realizing that the God of grace sent the Lord Jesus to this world to do all for sinners what we could not do for ourselves. It is knowing that Jesus lived the perfect life that God demands and received in His death on the cross the penalty that we deserve for our sins. It is being rich in faith, understanding that we cannot add anything to what Christ has done for sinners but can only receive it as a gift. It is being rich in humility, knowing that we are unworthy and undeserving of God's favor. It is being rich in righteousness, receiving through faith the righteousness of Christ that qualifies us to stand acceptably in the presence of God. It is to be rich in forgiveness, rejoicing in the fact that our sins are fully and completely forgiven by God through Christ. It is being rich in hope, which means those who have been forgiven eagerly look forward to that day in which they will be received into the glories of heaven.

Rich in grace! Rich in glory! Those are the true riches, and they belong to all who will receive the Lord Jesus Christ as their Lord and Savior.

-30-

From God's Word, the Bible...

These things I write to you, though I hope to come to you shortly; but if I am delayed, I write so that you may know how you ought to conduct yourself in the house of God, which is the church of the living God, the pillar and ground of the truth. And without controversy great is the mystery of godliness:

God was manifested in the flesh,
Justified in the Spirit,
Seen by angels,
Preached among the Gentiles,
Believed on in the world,
Received up in glory.

1 Timothy 3:14-16

Things I Miss

Since my retirement from the pastorate, my wife and I have had the opportunity to attend services in several churches. We have seen preachers in blue jeans and heard lots of strumming on guitars. In one service we saw a pastor leap on a table to demonstrate the meaning of faith. He told us that he would not have made the leap if he had not had faith in the table.

Then there was the youth pastor who demonstrated the power of God for us by bundling together a few sheets of paper and ripping apart the bundle.

One of the churches in our city made headlines in the newspaper by setting the world record for the time it took to fasten a man to a wall with duct tape. My wife and I read the article and were glad that we were not there!

Still further, we have read about preachers using various props to make their sermons more "authentic." One pastor offered a series of sermons on marital relations with a bed on the platform. Another preached a sermon from a motorboat to show his congregation that they must be willing to "get out of the boat" and engage in heroic exploits for God.

Our experiences in churches and what we have read about churches have served me well. They have made me acutely aware of things I miss.

I miss the sense of eternity. It is very easy to attend service after service these days and hear little or nothing about anything beyond this life. One could easily get the impression that this life lasts forever. Meanwhile the Bible constantly affirms that this life speeds by and will soon be over. What then?

I miss the gospel, which is the good news of what God has done in and through His Son, Jesus Christ, to prepare sinners for eternity. It is the good news of Christ taking our humanity, living without sin, dying a special kind of death (in which He received the wrath of God in the place of His people), and rising from the grave and ascending to the right hand of God. One could never guess from most sermons that Christianity was designed by God to rescue law-breaking, God-hating, judgment-facing sinners through the saving work of Jesus Christ. It is, rather, very easy to draw the conclusion that Christianity is something that merely helps people cope with the stresses, strains, and challenges of daily living.

I miss seriousness. I am weary of the seemingly boundless urge to create a sense of frivolity and hilarity in services. One would never know from observing many pastors these days that they are, according to the Apostle Paul, to be "grave" or "sober-minded" (1 Tim. 3:2)—that is, serious about serious things.

I miss prayer, real prayer, that is. Most public praying I hear is so shallow, light, and breezy that no one could possibly conclude that prayer can and should lay hold of God.

I miss the loud, robust singing of the great hymns of the

church that call us away from our self-centeredness and urge us to ponder God and be "lost in wonder, love and praise."

I miss the spirit of expectancy. I remember times in which God's people so looked forward to being in the house of God that they could hardly wait for services to begin.

I miss powerful, Spirit-anointed preaching. While I applaud the emphasis in recent years on expository preaching, I must say preaching is more than accurately explaining a passage of Scripture. It is possible to be straight as a gun barrel theologically, and just as empty.

I miss the reverence that is inevitably produced by the awareness that we are in the presence of God—and His is always a holy presence.

And I miss services in which the focus is on God alone instead of the constant parade of services that "recognize" policemen, firemen, community leaders, military veterans, current military personnel, and sports teams that have won championships.

I am constantly baffled by pastors and churches that feel it is necessary to have services that "honor America" even while this country plunges deeper and deeper into godlessness.

I'm sure many will respond to these things by saying: "Times are different." Yes, they are. But are they better?

In all the things I miss, I am nevertheless thankful that the Lord Jesus Christ is Head of the church and that, in the final state of glory, He, the Sovereign King, will receive all the honor and all the glory.

-31-

From God's Word, the Bible...

Behold what manner of love the Father has bestowed on us, that we should be called children of God! Therefore the world does not know us, because it did not know Him. Beloved, now we are children of God; and it has not yet been revealed what we shall be, but we know that when He is revealed, we shall be like Him, for we shall see Him as He is. And everyone who has this hope in Him purifies himself, just as He is pure.

1 John 3:1-3

Astonishing Love

The Apostle John begins this passage with an exclamation. It is an exclamation of astonishment.

John had seen more astonishing things than any man his age: Jesus healing the sick, casting out demons, stilling storms, feeding multitudes and even raising the dead. John was present on the mount when Jesus temporarily pulled back his robe of humanity so his heavenly glory could be seen. To top it all, John had also seen the risen Christ.

It would seem that John had seen so much that nothing could now astonish him. Not so! As an old man he still feels astonishment and expresses it here. And the thing that astonishes him is God's love. John calls us away from dull familiarity with that love.

John Cotton says: "The Apostle doth here correct our squint." Christians have a tendency to squint at the love of God. Let's carefully read John's words so we can completely open our eyes to see anew God's astonishing love.

What is it about that love that is so thrilling? John answers by pointing to two things.

What the love of God has already done
The love of God has bestowed on believers the title "children of God." John could lay claim to many titles: apostle, author of Scripture, pastor, but this one most thrilled him—child of God! And this is what he wanted his readers to be thrilled about—that they also could lay claim to the title "children of God."

But it was more than a title. It was a reality. So John, according to some translations, writes: "And so we are."

We will never appreciate this privilege as we should until we understand the incredibly wide chasm represented by two words in this text: "Father" and "us."

The Father is light without any hint of darkness at all (1:5). This means God is perfectly holy. And us? We are anything but holy! God has given us commands to obey, and we have broken every one, again and again.

This chasm is infinitely wide! We could not cross it, and God did not have to do anything to cross it! But here is His love—He did cross it in and through His Son, the Lord Jesus Christ. In love for sinners, God sent Jesus to live the life those sinners have refused to live, and to die the death they deserved to die.

Now on the basis on what Jesus did, God freely and gladly invites sinners everywhere to come to Christ and be saved, pardoned and forgiven.

John could not get over this love. So he exclaims: "What manner of love is this!" Literally translated, John writes: "From what country is this kind of love?" It is as if he is saying: "I am familiar with various kinds of love. I have a category for this kind and that kind, but I have no category for the love of God for sinners. It transcends all my categories."

What the love of God will yet do
That same love is going to take all of God's children into an unspeakably glorious future.

There is in verse two an intermingling of the uncertain and the certain. What is uncertain? John writes: "… it has not yet been revealed what we shall be…" (v.2). The full details about "what we shall be" have not been released yet. The future of the children of God will be of such a nature that the greatest flights of imagination of which we are now capable can get us nowhere near the total reality. What shall we be? We will have to wait and see!

But the uncertainty John expresses has to do only with the specific details. He is not expressing uncertainty about the future itself. To the contrary, he emphatically adds: "…but we know that when He is revealed, we shall be like Him, for we shall see Him as He is" (v.2).

God's children are not uncertain about Jesus coming again. That's in the blessed "we know" category. Furthermore, God's children are not uncertain about being like Him. That's also in the "we know" category.

Jesus is going to come for His people; they are going to see Him and be transformed into His likeness. Paul says: "For our citizenship is in heaven, from which we also eagerly wait for the Savior, the Lord Jesus Christ, who will transform our lowly body that it may be conformed to His glorious body, according to the working by which He is able even to subdue all things to Himself" (Phil. 3:20,21).

While these things are in the future, they significantly influence the present. This is the future with a present punch. So John adds: "And everyone who has this hope in Him, purifies himself, just as He is pure" (v.3). If by the grace of God we are anticipating future glory, we will make it our business to live holy lives in this present world.

About the Author

Roger Ellsworth is a retired pastor, active in ministry and writing, who lives in Jackson, Tennessee. He and his wife, Sylvia, love the message of the Bible, and they enjoy sharing the wonderful counsel of the Word of God in language that ordinary people can understand and appreciate.

Roger has written numerous books on the Christian faith, and has exercised a preaching ministry for over fifty years. His sermons are available to listen for free on SermonAudio.com.

Look for more books in this series from Roger. The next will include contributions from his wife and other members of their family.

More Books Coming Soon!

Enjoy collecting the *My Coffee Cup Meditations* series.

www.mycoffeecupmeditations.com

https://www.facebook.com/MyCoffeeCupMeditations/

www.ingramcontent.com/pod-product-compliance
Lightning Source LLC
Chambersburg PA
CBHW070623300426
44113CB00010B/1637